When the Spirit Speaks

When the Spirit Speaks

Touched by God's Word

Peter and Debbie Herbeck

PUBLISHED BY ST. ANTHONY MESSENGER PRESS
CINCINNATI, OHIO

Unless otherwise noted, Scripture passages have been taken from the *Revised Standard Version*, Catholic edition. Copyright ©1946, 1952, 1971 by the Division of Christian Education of the National Council of the Churches of Christ in the USA. Used by permission. All rights reserved. (Note: The editors of this volume have made minor changes in capitalization to some of the Scripture quotations herein. Please consult the original source for proper capitalization.)

Quotes are taken from the English translation of the *Catechism of the Catholic Church* for the United States of America (indicated as *CCC*), 2nd ed. Copyright ©1997 by United States Catholic Conference—Libreria Editrice Vaticana.

Cover design and photo by LUCAS Art & Design, Grandville, Michigan
Book design by Phillips Robinette, O.F.M.

LIBRARY OF CONGRESS CATALOGING-IN-PUBLICATION DATA

Herbeck, Peter.
  When the spirit speaks : touched by God's word / Peter and Debra Herbeck.
      p. cm.
  Includes bibliographical references.
  ISBN 978-0-86716-764-1 (pbk. : alk. paper) 1. Spirituality—Catholic Church. I. Herbeck, Debra. II. Title.

BX2350.65.H47 2007
248.4'82—dc22

                              2007000340

ISBN 978-0-86716-764-1

Published by Servant Books, an imprint of
St. Anthony Messenger Press.
28 W. Liberty St.
Cincinnati, OH 45202
www.AmericanCatholic.org
www.ServantBooks.org

Printed in the United States of America.
Printed on acid-free paper.

12 13 14 15   5 4 3 2

Contents

Foreword

One of the important contributions of Pope John Paul II in preparing the church for the challenges of the new millennium was to stress the importance of each Catholic's having a living relationship with God. He spoke of the purpose of his pontificate as being to help each Catholic become more "docile to the Holy Spirit."[1]

In his speech at the first worldwide meeting of renewal movements in the church in 1998, the pope underlined this emphasis in a particularly vivid way:

> The Church's self-awareness [is] based on the certainty that Jesus Christ is alive, is working in the present and changes life…. With the Second Vatican Council, the Comforter recently gave the Church…a renewed Pentecost, instilling a new and unforeseen dynamism.
>
> Whenever the Spirit intervenes, he leaves people astonished. He brings about events of amazing newness; he radically changes persons and history. This

was the unforgettable experience of the Second Vatican Ecumenical Council, during which, under the guidance of the same Spirit, the Church rediscovered the charismatic dimension as one of her constitutive elements: "It is not only through the sacraments and the ministrations of the Church that the Holy Spirit makes holy the people, leads them and enriches them with his virtues. Allotting his gifts according as he wills (cf. 1 Corinthians 12:11), he also distributes special graces among the faithful of every rank…. He makes them fit and ready to undertake various tasks and offices for the renewal and building up of the Church" (*Lumen Gentium,* n.12).

Pope John Paul II and his collaborators later reiterated this theme, and sometimes these exact words, as did Benedict XVI in the first initiative of his pontificate, as he convened a similar meeting.

With these words Pope John Paul II honestly acknowledged what many theologians, Scripture scholars and church historians had demonstrated in their studies: that the charismatic workings of the Holy Spirit are an essential and complementary reality to the sacramental and hierarchical dimensions of the church's existence. The pope also honestly acknowledged that the charismatic dimension, important as it is, nevertheless in a way was forgotten or overshadowed by perhaps a too exclusive emphasis on the sacramental and hierarchical. It required a special action of the Holy Spirit in the Second Vatican Council, the pope said, to bring the church back to an awareness of the importance of this "constitutive" dimension.

The pope went on to make this explicit:

> The institutional and charismatic aspects are co-essential as it were to the Church's constitution. They contribute, although differently, to the life, renewal and sanctification of God's People. It is from this providential rediscovery of the Church's charismatic dimension that before and after the Council, a remarkable pattern of growth has been established for ecclesial movements and new communities.... You, present here, are the tangible proof of this "outpouring" of the Spirit.

The Pope then made this extraordinary plea to all Christians, rising from his seat with difficulty as he did so:

> Today, I would like to cry out to all of you gathered here in St. Peter's Square and to all Christians: Open yourselves docilely to the gifts of the Spirit! Accept gratefully and obediently the charisms which the Spirit never ceases to bestow on us![2]

Peter and Debra Herbeck have performed a valuable service to the whole church in gathering these testimonies about how the words of John Paul II are coming to life in the church today. Jesus is truly alive, acting in the present, changing lives. The Spirit is truly at work, intervening in astonishing ways. The gifts of the Spirit are being poured out in abundance. This book provides the inspiring evidence of the truth of these words and an opportunity for all of us to encounter Christ in a deeper way and be ever more open to the wonderful work of the Spirit.

Ralph Martin

Director, Graduate Theology Program
in the New Evangelization

Sacred Heart Major Seminary

Archdiocese of Detroit

Introduction

A few summers ago I spent two weeks vacationing with my family in the mountains of Breckenridge, Colorado. It was a perfect spot to vacation—glorious, rugged mountains, deep blue skies and lots of quiet. The previous twelve months had been intense, packed with activity. I welcomed the time alone with my family and hoped to find enough quiet to get my spiritual battery recharged as well.

My interior clock was set on work time and Michigan time, so each day, especially the first week, I rose early while Debbie and the kids slept. It usually takes me a couple of weeks to wind down and to forget about all the responsibilities and deadlines that I tend to carry like a heavy weight on my shoulders when I'm worn out. The quiet of the early morning provided an ideal opportunity to pray and to reconnect with the Lord.

All I could say the first few days was, "I'm tired, Lord, and I feel spiritually flat. My well is dry, and I'm hoping you'll fill it up in these days. I'd really like it if you'd vacation with us and help us experience your presence." I dutifully read Scripture, but that mostly felt like work.

One morning, at the end of the first week, I woke up about five in the morning. Warm rays of bright sunlight were already breaking through cracks in the window shade. The room was perfectly still, and I could feel a powerful, peaceful presence in the room. I didn't see anything, but I knew that it was God. Unlike other times in my life when I've experienced the presence of the Lord, this time I had a very distinct feeling that God the Father was present. It seemed as if he was standing at the end of my bed, gazing at me with a look of satisfaction and delight.

I asked God, "Do you want to say something to me?" I didn't hear anything audible, but I knew that God was speaking to me: "Peter, it is good that you exist. I made you. You are my idea. And I have never had a bad idea."

As God spoke those words, I felt the weight being lifted off my shoulders. My heart began to fill with delight and pure joy. I wanted to get up and dance on my bed, but my wife was sleeping next to me.

For the rest of that vacation and for weeks after, I felt free as a child, unburdened from all the anxieties and concerns I had insisted upon carrying. I walked without a care in the world. In my heart I kept hearing the words, "It is good that you exist. You are my idea." I thought, "Yes, it is good that I exist! I'm not here by accident; I'm his idea. What am I worried about? Everything is going to be OK, because he's here with me, and he likes being here."

I've thought about that morning and the following weeks many times over in the past few years. A simple word from the Lord carried restorative power and energy to my soul. I felt physically refreshed and rested too. It continues to amaze me how a gentle touch from the Lord can lift burdens and speak truth to the human spirit.

King David, in Psalm 16, records his experience of hearing God's voice:

> I bless the LORD who gives me counsel;
> > in the night also my heart instructs me....
> Therefore my heart is glad, and my soul rejoices;
> > my body also dwells secure....
> You show me the path of life;
> > in your presence there is fulness of joy,
> > in your right hand are pleasures for evermore.
> > > (Psalm 16:7, 9, 11)

Jesus promised us that he would send us his Spirit: "But the Counselor, the Holy Spirit, whom the Father will send in my name, he will teach you all things" (John 14:26); "When the Spirit of truth comes, he will guide you into all the truth.... He will take what is mine and declare it to you" (John 16:13,14).

God, our Father, wants to speak to us. Jesus, our Lord, wants to guide us. He has died so that he could give us the promised Holy Spirit. That Spirit "comes to meet us" (*CCC*, 683) to "awaken faith" (*CCC*, 684), "to unite [us] to Christ and to make [us] live in him" (*CCC*, 690), to make it possible for us to "comprehend the thoughts of God" so that "we might understand the gifts bestowed on us by God" (1 Corinthians 2:11, 12), making us "God's temple" (1 Corinthians 3:16), bestowing genuine freedom (see 2 Corinthians 3:17) and "bearing witness with our spirit that we are children of God" (Romans 8:16).

The Christian life *is* a life in the Spirit. God calls every baptized person to "walk by the Spirit" (Galatians 5:16) and to "live by the Spirit" (Galatians 5:25). The Spirit comes ready to guide, to counsel, to encourage, to empower, to console, to liberate, to live with us and to walk with us. "You have been anointed by the Holy One…. The anointing which you received from him abides in you" (1 John 2:20, 27).

The anointing Jesus has given us is a reality, a truth that he wants us to experience. In fact, it's more accurate to say that this anointing is a person, the Holy Spirit, whom the Father and the Son want us to know and love. Jesus refers to this anointing as a baptism in the Holy Spirit (see Acts 1:5). This is our inheritance. To be Christian means to live in a conscious, personal relationship with God in the Holy Spirit.

The apostles had a conscious awareness that they were living under the guidance of the Spirit, and they expected the same confirming presence of the Spirit to be a reality in the life of every believer. Saint Paul referred to the Galatians as "you who are spiritual": that is, their life was characterized by the Spirit. The experience of the Spirit was not limited to elect individuals. It was part of the normal Christian life. Saint Paul exhorted the Corinthians to desire the spiritual gifts—prophecy, tongues, healing and so on (see 1 Corinthians 12:29–31; 14).

This experience is also part of normal Christian life today. Father Kilian McDonnell, author, theologian and Benedictine monk, quoting a German theologian, states: "Experience of the Spirit is not merely one aspect of the new life of the believing community, it is the principle of it."[1]

Yet for many baptized Christians, the Spirit is a doctrine to be believed, the overlooked Third Person of the Trinity, not a reality of personal experience. The lively expectation of living with the Spirit so characteristic of the lives of the apostles is overshadowed by the hardened secularist rationalism that characterizes our culture. What's real is what can be measured repeatedly. The "experience" of the Spirit falls outside those parameters, so it is often met with suspicion and skepticism. Yet, as Father McDonnell puts it, "the modern critical reserve concerning such an experience of the Spirit should not obscure the fact that early Christianity was convinced of it."[2]

Debbie and I have been privileged to witness this outpouring of the Holy Spirit in our local community and beyond. With joy we bring you this collection of stories of ordinary people, young and old, rich and poor, who like the apostles are convinced that the Holy Spirit has touched and changed their lives.

Some of these stories come from members of the Catholic charismatic parish to which we belong; others come from women in a local branch of a Bible study, for which Debbie was a teaching director. Still others come from people whom we have encountered through Renewal Ministries, the Catholic renewal organization with which we are involved. We have also been active in youth ministry, and we now have four teenage children of our own, so we have devoted a chapter to stories of youth who have experienced God in a personal, life-changing way.

Some of these stories are dramatic; some include instances of particular gifts and manifestations of the Spirit, such as speaking in tongues, falling down or "resting in the Spirit," prophecy and words of knowledge. Others are simple accounts of the quite ordinary ways the Spirit is at work today. All convey a living expectation that the promises of Jesus are true. The men and women behind them expect and anticipate the action of the Spirit in their lives. They have learned to "walk by the Spirit" (Galatians 5:16).

Jesus said, "I am with you always, to the end of the age" (Matthew 28:20). Those words become a reality through the experience of the Holy Spirit. Jesus promised to send comfort, counsel, consolation, power and much, much more. May these stories inspire you to seek more of the Holy Spirit's action and presence in your life.

CHAPTER ONE

The Spirit as the Source of New Life

To set the mind on the Spirit is life.

Romans 8:6

Fire, Spirit and the Eucharist

—Carolyn from Michigan

My life with the Lord has been one largely marked by his leading. It is, therefore, not at all strange to me that my baptism in the Spirit should come by much the same route: Jesus' leading, my accepting the action of the Holy Spirit in my life, followed by divine appointments that helped to identify the experience after the fact.

It began one spring about ten years ago with a commitment I made to the Lord. On my twenty-eighth birthday I decided to make daily Mass attendance a part of my spiritual life. This choice came on the heels of my reentry into the Catholic church, largely brought about by recognition of the true presence of Jesus in the Eucharist.

Returning to the Catholic church was not an easy task. I gave up many close friends and my first experience of community, the place where I had shared my Christian walk with others who had the same understanding and zeal for Christian living and discipleship. However, I trusted in the Lord's protection and provision, and I recognized the incredible gift of Jesus' real and actual presence in the Eucharist. I knew in the depths of my being that I could survive without fellowship, but I could never live without the Eucharist.

So I made a decision to attend daily Mass to honor the Lord and to gratefully accept the incredible gift he makes available to us every day. There was no motive for my actions other than to put the Lord first in my life and trust that he would provide and take care of me in return. Little did I know what he had in store for me.

After about five weeks of attending daily Mass, something began to happen after receiving the Eucharist. My soul would be lifted up literally to heaven, where the Lord would bring his Spirit to mine in a way I had not experienced previously. I was not frightened by the power of the Lord coming upon me; rather I opened myself up and took it all in, much as a wilted flower might delight in a refreshing waterfall.

Shortly after these experiences began, I started to pray in a new and strange way. I was praying in a foreign tongue, one I neither recognized nor had studied. I did not fight this because I did not want to impede what the Lord was doing in me. Indeed, this experience of the Holy Spirit so encompassed my being that I did not want it to stop. I later learned that the gift of tongues is one of the gifts the Holy Spirit gives to his people, as in Acts 2.

These precious moments after receiving the Eucharist brought a new presence, a new power of the Lord in my life. The communion I experienced with the Trinity still takes my breath away to this day.

A sister who worked in the parish office approached me one day after Mass. She said she had noticed something happening with me after Communion, and she wondered if we could talk about it. I felt a bit odd sharing such an intimate experience, particularly one for which I had few words of explanation. I thought she might think I was crazy. Sister Lucille, however, "just happened" to be one of the leaders of the charismatic prayer group at my parish.

Soon I found myself in Sister Lucille's office sharing about my journey with Christ and my return to the church and struggling to explain what was happening to me. Sister Lucille's face lit up. When I finished my story, she leapt out of her chair, threw her arms around me and proclaimed that I had been baptized in the Spirit.

Sister asked if she could invite the parish business manager to come in so that the two of them could pray over me. As they prayed, a peace settled deep in my soul, telling me that I was home. After that I began to use this new way of praying in my daily life. I attended a Life in the Spirit Seminar, an introductory class to the power of the Holy Spirit and his gifts, which included an opportunity for prayer for the baptism in the Holy Spirit.

Fire and Spirit—this is what we eat when we receive the Eucharist. The Creator, the Lord of heaven and earth, desires to give us himself to feast on—daily if we choose—so that he can use *us* to build his kingdom. What an awesome discovery: Jesus chooses me to love and help him and does not leave me unaided, for he gives me his very self to do the task. The Eucharist is a sign of his life, his animating Spirit.

A Fighter Pilot and the Rosary

—Joe from Missouri

I am a cradle Catholic. My parents were very serious Catholics, and they sacrificed a lot to have all of us go to Catholic schools. I attribute much of my deep conversion to the example they lived.

I grew up in the sixties, and in high school I concentrated on sports. I became involved in drugs and drinking at an early age. As I matured, I knew I had to give up these ways.

I was about to graduate from college when I realized that I could pursue a lifelong dream to fly airplanes. I went cold turkey to get off the drugs. Not long after that I applied to the Air Force and was accepted as an officer and a pilot. During my first year in the military, I married my best friend.

Life was pretty good. I was a newlywed in pilot training in the Air Force. Within a year my wife was pregnant with our first child.

We always went to Mass every Sunday, but I don't remember going to confession. Since I had been separated geographically from my wife for most of our engagement, we never had discussed contraception in a serious setting, and as a result we never understood the church's teaching. We were carried away with the rest of the contraceptive culture. We were "cafeteria" Catholics, picking and choosing the teachings of the church that suited our desires. Over the years it became apparent to me that my wife could not go on taking the pill because of the obvious side effects. In the early nineties we decided that it would be OK for me to be sterilized. I actually thought we were dealing responsibly with our health issues and overpopulation. Many men I knew were doing this. I was like a dead fish floating down the river with other dead fish. But Jesus can raise men from the dead!

As an A-10 pilot in the Air Force, flying in two wars and being deployed to southwest Asia gave me much time to reflect. I was shot at, and I shot at people in combat. I certainly lived most of my fighter pilot days as if I were bulletproof. That came to an end very gently but powerfully through the intercession of our Blessed Mother.

In the 1980s I was flying training missions and fighting the Cold War throughout Europe. The Iron Curtain was up then, and our unit was prepared to take heavy losses should the Soviets ever invade West Germany. It was then that my dad handed me his rosary. Little did I know that he was handing me the best weapon against the most deadly enemy I faced— not flesh and blood but principalities and powers.

I carried that rosary with me on every mission I flew, but it was not until after the Gulf War in 1991 that I finally began to pray it. God's grace had begun to penetrate my granite heart while I was deployed in Kuwait and flying support missions over Iraq. Now my twenty years in the service were coming to an end, and I had to transition to civilian life.

Deep within me I knew that my sterilization was a grave sin, and I went to confession. During confession I cried a lot. After receiving absolution I knew that something was different, though nothing felt different. I know now that I was being drawn by the Immaculate Heart of Mary to her Son.

Very gently but deliberately I began to desire to learn more about my Catholic faith. The Lord put people and events in my life to help me.

I always had wondered why Protestants had so much fervor. Within a week I had a conversation with a parishioner who was a convert from Protantism, and he gave me a book about the

Catholic faith. Reading this book began such an intense desire for knowledge of the faith that at times I would cry from frustration. I had wasted so much time, and there was so much beauty to know! I deeply desired the Eucharist and began to pray the rosary every day.

We moved to Missouri, and I went to work for United Airlines. The transition was difficult after being in a single-seat fighter my whole career. But after some rough times, things worked out. We joined the parish I grew up in, and our two children enrolled in confirmation classes.

In May 2002 at a Saturday vigil mass, my children were confirmed. During the recessional hymn, as the bishop walked past me down the center aisle, I encountered something new. What I can only describe as a supernatural embrace overwhelmed me. This feeling enveloped my whole body from top to bottom and immobilized me in the process. Uncontrollable tears came, and I sat down and then knelt down.

The church was almost empty, and my wife wanted to know what the matter was. All I could say was that I didn't know. I could not move. I finally just gave up and sat there crying. There I was—this big, tough ex-fighter pilot—weeping in the pew for no apparent reason.

In my heart I knew what was happening: Our God had lowered himself to embrace me, one of his sons, just as he lowers himself throughout the world at every moment in every Mass. I can never deserve him or ever repay him. Yet I know that we are all called to enter into this relationship with our Lord, to love him and to desire to please him above all things!

Alone But Never Lonely
—Vince from Canada

One Saturday morning in 1970, my wife Lucy and I went to a hotel in Toronto to attend a Full Gospel Business Men's Fellowship breakfast. We did not know anything about this association, but a priest had advised us to go. We both felt like strangers there.

One young actor gave his testimony, telling us that he had been fired from the Stratford Festival and wanted to commit suicide, but his friends had brought him to a previous breakfast where a speaker, Kevin Ranaghan, prayed for him. His life was completely changed.

I had seen Kevin Ranaghan's book *Catholic Pentecostals* in a Catholic bookstore, but it seemed contradictory to me. I thought, "If I am Catholic, how can I be a Pentecostal?" After hearing the actor's testimony, I went out and bought that book. I read the stories of how the Holy Spirit had come upon students at Duquesne University during a retreat in 1967, which initiated the beginning of the charismatic renewal in the Catholic church.

I took the book with me on a business trip to

Windsor, Ontario. Reading the testimonies in my motel room, I became really hungry for God. I wanted to have the same experience as those students. That night I turned the light off, put the book on the table, knelt beside the bed and started praying aloud. I prayed in English and Lithuanian, my native tongue.

First I asked the Lord to forgive me for any way I had hurt my wife and my children, and suddenly I was afraid. But right away I said to myself, "I know where I am, and I know what I am doing." After praying for about five minutes, I felt complete relief from my fear, and the presence of the Holy Spirit filled the room. Everything changed, and I rejoiced.

The next morning as I was driving home, the sun was shining in my eyes, and I felt sleepy, wanting a cup of coffee. I shouted, "Oh, Holy Spirit!" At that moment I felt strong power going through my body; it was just like touching live electrical wires. I began praising God and singing, and after a while I realized that I was praying in a language I did not know.

When I arrived home I told the story to my wife. Four months later she had the same experience. I also shared this with a seminarian friend, who is now a priest. As I finished describing my experience, I said, "This is the end of my story." He answered, "No, this is just the beginning."

And it was! Thirty-five years later, through the grace of God, I feel the same fire in my heart as I felt on June 21, 1970.

We began a prayer meeting in our home, and it later developed into a prayer group. I organized a small men's prayer group, and for eighteen years we met on Saturday mornings for an hour of prayer, praise, repentance and intercession. I've heard it said that "it is easier to obtain than to maintain." Thank God, we did not let the fire of the Holy Spirit die.

Every year I go back to my native Lithuania for four weeks and preach to various groups (mainly young people) and lead them to Jesus. The Holy Spirit is working. He has changed our family.

My wife is now with the Lord, after suffering with bone cancer. People used to ask her, "What keeps you going?" She never said a word; she would just point to the crucifix.

Today I live alone, but I am never lonely.

A Fire That Did Not Burn
—Steve from Canada

When I was a teenager, I began to question many things about the church, Jesus and the meaning of life. I had made up my mind to determine one way or another if Jesus was really who he said he was or if it was all a sham, designed to keep people in line. I decided that if it were false, I would leave the Catholic church and never set foot in another church for the rest of my life.

Lying in bed one night after going to confession, I said a prayer something like, "Jesus, I am cleansed now. Will you accept me into your kingdom?" At once the presence of the Holy Spirit filled me with great joy.

Up until that point I had felt like a dead man with no sense of what real love and joy were. Now I knew for sure that Jesus was who he said he was, and I knew the Holy Spirit lived too, because the fire of his love burned within my heart.

A few weeks later I was lying in my bed praying when suddenly the Holy Spirit entered my room. It's a little difficult to describe the experience, but I could "see" the Holy Spirit, not with my eyes but rather with my heart, mind and spirit. The Holy Spirit was like a ball of tumbling flames—red and orange and rolling. He was full of great power and yet so full of gentleness. The Spirit was like a cool fire that did not burn, like the burning bush before Moses.

I knew in my spirit that I was in God's great presence, so I said, "Lord, what do you want of me?"

He said, "Ask me for the gift of tongues."

So I replied, "Lord, I ask you for the gift of tongues."

At once a flame leapt out from the tumbling ball of fire and struck me in the stomach. I could feel the power of the Holy Spirit within me, traveling up my body toward my mouth. When it reached my tongue, I began speaking in tongues. It was awesome, to say the least.

I stayed up for many hours, cupping my hands to my mouth and ear so that I could hear what I was saying in tongues. Of course, I couldn't understand what I was saying, but it was a sign of God's presence with me and has been ever since. I am now forty-four years old, and I am praying for the gift of the interpretation of tongues and prophecy.

I believe the Holy Spirit wants to pour out his gifts upon his church. He only waits for us to ask for them.

From Head to Heart
—Helen from Minnesota

My husband and I have four children, whom we taught and raised to know and appreciate the values and principles of our Catholic faith. After they grew up and left, there seemed to be a void in my life. A friend invited me to come to a course in evangelization at our parish.

It was during this course that I began to discover how "stale" my faith had become. Gradually the head knowledge of my faith was transformed, and it began to fill that hole in my heart. I began to feel and see the power of the Holy Spirit in my life. Others began to notice the change and commented on it to me.

I had been ill with lupus for the previous eighteen years. My rheumatologist noticed an improvement in my health. He ordered blood tests, and they confirmed that my lupus was in remission.

I began to see many other manifestations of the gifts of the Holy Spirit in my life. A daughter-in-law came to the evangelization course, and then God's amazing love brought back a wayward son. I see the Holy Spirit's action in my love of the sacraments, hunger for the Scriptures, longing for praise and worship and other empowering gifts of the Holy Spirit that are now present in our parish and in our community.

Who's in Charge?

—Jackie from Michigan

In 1992 I was living my dream life. I was married to the man of my dreams, we had a beautiful one-year-old daughter, and I had a promising career in banking. We decided it was time for a second child. What I didn't know was that God had decided it was time for me to begin a journey that would change my life.

During the next two years I had four miscarriages, and by the end of that time I was on the verge of an emotional breakdown. I had never faced tragedy, so I didn't know how to grieve. Even worse, my faith was very weak. Although I had been raised Catholic, my husband and I only went to church when it was convenient.

I knew God was out there, watching over me, but I had been taught that I was in control of my life and that it was my responsibility to be a useful member of society—to be good and work hard. I was doing all that, so why were these bad things happening?

My doctor gave me a little bottle of pills to "calm my nerves." On the outside I appeared to be functioning, but inside I had a hole in my heart that I couldn't fix, and I felt helpless.

A friend suggested that I go with her to a nondenominational women's Bible study. As I listened to the speaker there, the Word came alive. I never had imagined that God wanted a relationship with me. I started reading Christian books and listening to Christian radio.

I began to feel a little uncomfortable being Catholic. My Protestant friends told me about all of the things Catholics did and believed that went against biblical teaching. I started attending a Protestant church, and I couldn't believe how excited and in love with the Lord these Christians were. This style of worship was very different from what I had witnessed at my Catholic church.

One day I was reading an article by a priest about Catholics leaving the church when it hit me: I was about to leave something I knew nothing about. I felt strongly in my heart that God wanted me to search for the truth, and I obeyed.

Shortly after my quest began, a Catholic friend invited me to a Catholic rally in Detroit. I had no idea what to expect, but I knew I needed to go. There, much to my surprise, I saw hundreds of Catholics praising and worshiping the Lord with their hands held high. These folks truly were on fire with the

Spirit of the Lord. I sang, I cried, and I knew I was on the path to finding truth and healing.

I read everything and listened to everything I could about the Catholic faith. I prayed often and found God leading me to pass on what I was learning.

Eventually I wanted to try leading a Bible study for Catholic adults. That summer I attended a school of Catholic Bible study to get all the information I needed to get started. I was bringing my plan before God, wanting him to bless it. I received much more than information. I sang, I prayed, I cried and I felt renewed. I also knew it was not the time to start a Bible study. God had other plans, and I couldn't wait to find out what they were!

Four months later my husband came across an ad in the newspaper. A nearby parish was looking for a director of religious education. He was certain I should apply. I was shocked. I had worked at a bank for seventeen years and was an assistant vice president. I was well respected and worked hard.

But I knew I wasn't happy there. My family was willing to sacrifice the big changes a job switch would mean for them. So I applied and received the position of director of religious education.

This job is a gift from God. I love what I do! I am also using everything I learned at the Bible study school, as I am now leading an adult Bible study.

At a time when I was ready to leave a "boring, stuffy old Catholic church," the Holy Spirit helped me discover an exciting relationship with God in a place

I never had expected! I always thought I was in control of my life, but the Spirit has been always with me.

No Point in Living

—Bob from Minnesota

On April 27, 2003, my youngest son, Matthew, and I were on our way to church when we came upon a car accident. I stopped to see if everything was OK. I was informed that my eldest son, Christopher, who was seventeen years old, had been involved in the accident while driving my truck. I was told that I should go to the hospital because it didn't look good.

Up to that point I hadn't considered myself a very religious person. I went to church, but I really didn't practice my faith. On the way to the hospital we prayed out loud that everything would be OK, but inside I prayed that God's will would be done. I also prayed that I would be able to hold Christopher one last time.

I will never forget the moment I walked down the hallway in the emergency room and heard the doctor tell me that my son was gone. There had been nothing else that they could do.

As June began I felt like a failure. I hadn't been there to protect Christopher, and I had let my entire family down. I thought to myself, "What is the reason for being here?" I felt so lost that I just didn't want to live anymore. So I picked the place and method to kill myself; I just didn't know when I was going to do it.

In July I found myself driving to work one day and just screaming at God, "WHY? You said in the Bible, 'Ask anything in my name, and it will be done,' and I asked to hold my son one more time." Why couldn't God hold up his end of the deal? I just didn't understand.

A few days later, when I got to work, I had to walk to the other end of my job site, which was about three blocks long, to check on things. On my way back I felt someone behind me. Figuring it was one of my crew, I turned around, but no one was there.

At that same moment I felt as if somebody was picking me up under my arms and helping me to walk. As I looked down I couldn't feel the ground, even though my feet were on the ground. I knew right away that it was JESUS carrying me! I felt so much love and peace that I knew everything would be all right. In that moment he changed my heart and instilled in me a love for him that is strong and everlasting!

This experience was so overwhelming that all I could say was, "Thank you, Jesus," over and over again. Finally my prayer was answered, and I knew I would hold my son again in heaven. Jesus had more than answered my prayer; he showed me that I must live for him. Not only had he saved my life, but also I now understood that he had died to save my soul so that I could be with God forever.

Ninety-one and Full of Joy

—Agnes from Ohio

One day back in 1960, I looked at the TV schedule and saw a program coming on called *The 700 Club.* I thought it was going to be a nightclub with singing and dancing. I was surprised to see it was a Christian show. As I watched it for a few minutes, I was amazed to hear the people talk about Jesus as though they personally knew him. They talked about the Holy Spirit actually working in their lives.

I knew about Jesus, and I knew about the Holy Spirit. But as I sat watching these people, I knew that they had something I did not, and I wanted it.

My parents were the old-fashioned kind. They came to America from Slovakia. They went to church every Sunday and every holy day. They were strict about Lent—fasting and going to services every Wednesday and Friday evening and Sunday after-noon—as well as Easter and Christmas observances. It was a way of life, doing what God, through the Catholic church, told us to do. It was not a harsh life, because we were always told that God loves us.

Shortly after watching *The 700 Club,* a lady I met in our church parking lot told me that there was a prayer group at the Byzantine church a block away. There were four or five people from our church already going there, so I went. Although I did not understand it at the time, as I was walking down the steps to the door of the hall where the group was meeting, I had a feeling that I was coming home.

The meeting was amazing. The priest and all of the people were filled with the Spirit—praising God, praying, speaking in tongues. It was beautiful; God was with us.

One night after my second or third meeting, I came home and lay down in bed. All of a sudden I saw over my head the group of people in a circle, just as we had sat at the prayer meeting, and over the circle of people appeared a dove, the symbol of the Holy Spirit. As I watched this I felt a flood of love wash over me, a love so sweet and pure that I could not explain the feeling. It was absolutely beyond description.

A few days later, still pondering what had happened and wondering if I had dreamt it, I was vacuuming the living room when suddenly that same love swept over me again. I am convinced it was our Lord telling me, "Yes, it was me."

I thank God and praise him every day, and I surrender to his will each day. Now I know that he did not drop us off here on earth and say, "Good luck. I'll see you on the other side." I know we can have a personal relationship with him right here, right now.

I am now ninety-one years old. I had to have my left leg amputated, but I am still praising God with all my heart, spirit and soul. Even now he is blessing me. He has sent seven people from my parish to help me. I live alone, but with the help they give me I am very comfortable. My life is full of joy because he loves me.

I Knew That Christianity Was Not True
—Marsha from Michigan

Although I was raised in a nominally Christian household, God and church seemed to be for Sundays, not for the rest of the week. I did receive religious instruction growing up, but by the time I reached graduate school, it seemed to me that God and religion were not necessary for my life—or for anyone else's either.

The world clearly needed some fixing, and changing society politically seemed like the right avenue. During the first year of my doctoral studies at the University of Michigan, I was involved in politics through student organizations. However, that following summer of 1968, after the deaths of Martin Luther King, Jr., and Robert Kennedy, politics no longer seemed to be a foolproof option.

That first year I had become friends with a neighbor (who turned out to be a drug dealer). His regular challenges to the vestiges of my Christian ethical system became successful when I realized I had no sure foundation for any moral system. What if he was right that everyone needed to "look out for number one" and I was wrong to want to "be nice to people"? The two conflicting systems could not both be true, and both might even be false.

I understood that I needed to discover the truth so as not to go through life a naïve fool, but I had no idea how to start. The only thing I knew for sure was that Christianity was not true. The remaining options were infinite and confusing. I decided to stay in my apartment—with no social contact so as to avoid interference by any outside voices—until I had a foundation of sorts by which to make decisions and live my life.

After a few days of reading random passages out of many books with no success, I decided to open the Bible, which I had kept as a reference for my literary studies. I was hoping to come across some generic wisdom that I could use to help build some system of truth.

When I opened to Matthew 13:13, about having eyes and not seeing and ears and not hearing, I was catapulted instantly—and very much to my surprise—into the spiritual realm, which I did not know was even there. I became immediately aware that there was a God, Jesus Christ was his Son, and the Bible was not a "nice book" but the very Word of that holy God. Satan and his kingdom were real, and all the activity on earth was actually a struggle over the souls of human beings.

I experienced God as being truly alive and substantial, while I and everything around me were shadowy and flimsy. I had to rethink every category of life; I had to review, reevaluate and reassemble all of my experiences up to that point.

Because I had been in such mental and moral darkness, it took time to rebuild my life and grow in truth and righteousness, but over the years it has been a wonderful path. Knowing and loving God, and living for him, is the only satisfying life, because he is the Truth for every human being. I will forever be grateful to God for his sovereign action in my life, which removed me from the path of destruction I had chosen for myself and transplanted me into his kingdom.

Not in the Family Picture
—Eric from Minnesota

I considered myself a Christian most of my life. I knew about God and the gift of his Son for our salvation. I was active in the church and tried to live a "good" life. I had even experienced a personal relationship with God through Jesus Christ. But I never really had understood the role of the Holy Spirit in my life. As a result I slowly drifted away from that personal relationship.

I worked hard to maintain control of my life, but the harder I worked, the bigger mess my life became. My business was failing, debts were soaring, my marriage was struggling, my wife and I had a miscarriage, and my best friend committed suicide.

As these difficulties occurred, I simply worked even harder. Soon I was working three jobs, sixty to seventy hours per week. Before long I was spending all my waking time worrying about where I was going to earn my next dollar. This stress led to frequent anxiety attacks and waking at night in a sweat.

On the rare occasion when I wasn't working, my son would ask, "Why is Daddy coming with us?" One day, looking at photos, I realized I was not in any of our family pictures. I was always at work. I also realized that my son was growing up, and I didn't really know who he was.

When I saw how the chaos of my life was affecting my family, I swallowed my pride and began praying regularly to God to have mercy on my wife and son and bring peace to their lives. I didn't pray for my own peace, because I felt I deserved the misery I was experiencing.

Over the next year and a half God began answering my prayers. I found myself working one job and spending more time with my family. Despite working less, God created amazing circumstances that greatly reduced our debt, we moved into a nicer home, and we were blessed with our second son. I opened my heart a crack, and God showed me how much he cared for and loved me.

Yet I continued to suffer from anxiety and depression. I knew there had to be more to life. I knew I didn't deserve peace in my life but that God was willing to bring me peace. I knew my heart was hard, but I was unsure why.

Looking for the answer, I decided to attend a meeting at our church with my wife. I confessed to her the unknown obstacle between God and me. That night I found myself surrounded by people who were full of God's love, joy and peace. I felt as if God was trying to reach out to me, but an impenetrable wall was keeping me from communicating with him.

Driving home that night, God suddenly and vividly revealed himself to me. I knew instantly that the obstacle between God and me was my guilt: guilt over my failed business, over lying to others, over a struggling marriage and most of all over my friend's suicide. Just in that revelation I felt a huge weight lift from my shoulders. However, my heart still needed to be softened before I was ready to surrender completely to God.

Over the next few weeks, by the grace of the Holy Spirit, I was able to allow God to peel away the hard layers of my heart, and I let go of my guilt, piece by piece. On March 6, 2004, I allowed the last of my guilt to be nailed to the cross and to die an eternal death with Jesus Christ. The Holy Spirit filled my heart and overwhelmed me with God's love, peace and joy.

I finally understood the role of the Holy Spirit as a guiding power source in my life. No longer did I have to rely on head knowledge of God and his teaching in a trudge through life. I could now rely on God's eternal guiding spirit to be with me at all times and to bless me with many gifts to accomplish his special purpose for my life.

I no longer try to control my life. I know God has a specific purpose for me, and he reveals that purpose every day. I have a wife to love as Christ loves the church. I have two awesome boys with whom I can share my faith every day. I have a Father in heaven who is a model for my fatherly relationship with my boys. And I have a job where I can share my faith in Jesus Christ with my coworkers and clients on a regular basis.

I often start my day with a simple prayer that God will help me recognize the people and opportunities that he places before me. I am always amazed how easy it is to recognize those special people he places in my path and to respond to his calling. My life has been transformed.

God has answered my prayers by bringing peace into my heart. He continues to soften my heart and teach me how to surrender control of every aspect of my life to him. I now experience the overwhelming joy and peace that I previously thought were impossible. I'm finally living the Spirit-filled life God intended for me.

No More Angry Edge

—Lorraine from New Brunswick, Canada

I was brought up in a good Catholic family. While I was growing up, I always felt alone, as if I didn't belong. There was an awful pain and emptiness inside.

In my early twenties I left the church for a year or two, but eventually I came back. I married a non-Catholic, and we brought up our two children in the Catholic faith.

When my first child was born, I suffered a mental depression that lasted about nine months. I couldn't understand myself anymore, as I felt confused, afraid and out of control inside. I was absolutely petrified of my own baby and didn't know why.

Outwardly people thought I was fine, despite the terrible battle going on inside. I was blessed with a husband who never criticized me and seemed to accept the fact that I was doing my best. And I truly was trying to be a good mother.

After I had my second child, only eighteen months after my first, I began to look for solutions in the world because my pain and fears were so great. I began using birth control. Later I had a miscarriage after three months of being pregnant. In order to keep my sanity, I went to work for a while.

After a year or so, I felt that it was time for me to get back home with the children. But in order to cope, I began to dedicate myself to church work. Since I was driven to do things to perfection, I became very successful.

In about 1980 the parish began a Scripture study course that would last four years. I faithfully went to all these sessions. Out of this came a deep longing for more of God. I had studied God's Word, but I felt there had to be more. I wanted to pray with the Word, but I didn't know how.

One day, as I was doing the altar care in church, I

spoke from my heart to Jesus present in the tabernacle. I said something like, "Jesus, this is your church! Is it only about working and gathering for Sunday Mass? You're God! There's got to be more that you came to do! I want to know!"

Shortly afterward, in Lent of 1984, I attended a lecture series called "Women in the Church." I didn't know it, but there were women from a prayer group among us. I shared with the women there that I was praying to the Holy Spirit to lead me to where I should serve in the church.

A lady from this prayer group gently placed her hands on my arm and assured me that God would answer my prayers. Little did she know that God was choosing to answer me right then and there. As she spoke I had an image of beams of light radiating into me, and I felt I was receiving a most beautiful gift. There followed another image, that of the word *charismatic* written out.

A few weeks later the Lord Jesus released his Holy Spirit in me by simply exploding my heart with his love. I began attending the prayer group meetings. I took a Life in the Spirit Seminar, followed by a course on basic Christian maturity. I had a strong sense that Jesus was taking me on a journey with him for a reason I didn't know. I knew that he had a purpose for my life.

The Holy Spirit became real to me and began to guide and empower me to follow Jesus. Jesus gave me the gift of prayer and faithfulness to it. Through the Holy Spirit he clearly revealed to me that coming to him daily and praying with his holy Word was one of the main ways he was going to come to me in a deep and personal way.

The Eucharist and the sacrament of reconciliation had always been important to me, but the Holy Spirit helped me to see Jesus far more clearly in these sacraments. They became central to my life in a new and deeper way.

The first thing that Jesus did for me was to heal and forgive me for the way I had denied my woman-hood. Then the process of healing my motherhood began. During this time Jesus brought me to his mother Mary to help heal painful memories from when I was a baby. Jesus healed the feeling of being alone, too.

The Lord has set me free. I no longer feel this angry edge inside of me. I can now, by God's grace, move in compassion and love rather than from a center of fear and anger. I can allow people to touch me with their love, and I can know that I'm lovable. I feel acceptable for who I am.

CHAPTER TWO

God Is Calling Youth

*I will pour out my Spirit upon all flesh,
and your sons and your daughters
shall prophesy,
and your young men shall see visions.*

Acts 2:17

More Fun Than Beating Mortal Kombat

—Michael from Michigan, age eighteen

I was exposed to the Holy Spirit at a young age.
Parishioners at my church would speak freely in
tongues and use other gifts of the Holy Spirit. But I
didn't understand who the Holy Spirit was, nor did I
experience him for myself.

I went through a Life in the Spirit Seminar in fifth
grade and confirmation preparation in seventh
grade. At a prayer meeting in ninth grade, people
prayed over me for the gift of tongues, and I was able
to use it. But I still did not understand the Person and
power of the Holy Spirit, nor how that power could
work in my life.

Two summers ago at a Christian camp, one of the counselors gave a talk, then invited anyone who wanted prayer to come to the front of the room. I felt something inside pulling me to get prayed over, so I went up. As I was being prayed over, I just told God, "My heart is open to you; send your Holy Spirit upon me." Immediately the Holy Spirit came and filled my heart. I started feeling really hot, and a deep burning sensation came over my heart.

Then God showed me all of my friends, all of my loved ones, who had fallen away from him by doing sinful things. He was telling me, "These children of mine are lost, and I need you to help bring them back to me." I finally understood how powerful the Holy Spirit was and how he could work through my life.

The Holy Spirit had shown me that I needed to help my friends, but I knew I could not do it on my own. Sometimes I would shrug off the Holy Spirit's call because I was too afraid to act on it. But no matter how I tried to forget about it, I couldn't. There was always a nagging feeling in the pit of my stomach, reminding me of my call.

Some of the friends whom I was supposed to help would tell me proudly of their sins, as if they were accomplishments. This would eat me up inside. I knew that I needed to tell them that what they were doing was wrong, but I never seemed to get the chance. Then God provided the perfect opportunity.

My high school class went on a senior retreat. The retreat was an amazing opportunity to talk to some of my friends about God. I saw the Holy Spirit at work as he moved through my fellow students. The Holy Spirit dramatically changed some of their lives.

After the retreat one of the teachers started a Life in the Spirit Seminar, where he taught us about the Holy Spirit and the gifts of the Spirit. In the seminar I had the opportunity to pray over some of my friends who wanted to receive the gift of the Holy Spirit. This was the most amazing experience I've ever had— more exhilarating than being at a Notre Dame-USC football game, more fun than riding four-wheelers in Alaska and more rewarding than beating the *Mortal Kombat* video game!

I never expected it, but I have seen the Holy Spirit move in our school. He has changed not only my life but also the lives of many of my friends and family. The great thing about the Holy Spirit is that he is a gift. All we have to do is ask, and God will give the Spirit to us.

Me a Priest?

—Jim from Michigan, age eighteen

This past year I considered myself a normal high school senior. I had worked throughout my high school career just to be accepted and liked by my classmates, and it finally seemed as if my peers thought I was cool. I started the year as the quarterback and captain of the football team and was part of the homecoming court, I thought things were going great.

I had encountered the Holy Spirit in a personal way already, but I wanted some time for myself. I decided to put God on the back burner for senior year. But God had a different plan.

About a month into the school year, a newly ordained priest came to say Mass at our school. I was participating in Mass when I looked up at the priest and heard a voice say, "This is what I want you to do." Immediately I felt sick to my stomach. Me a priest? I had thought about the priesthood before but had always come to the conclusion that it was not for me.

I didn't tell any of my friends about what I had heard God say, because I was afraid of what they would think. I wanted to have control of my life, so I continued to try to ignore God. I kept doing all the things I thought a cool high school senior would do. But I just wasn't happy anymore. I felt emptiness in my heart. I felt as if I was carrying a heavy burden.

The Holy Spirit did not abandon me when I chose to ignore him the first time; instead he reached out to me. I was reading my Bible and wondering what God had planned for me when I stumbled across Matthew 11:28–30: "Come to me, all who labor and are heavy laden, and I will give you rest. Take my yoke upon you, and learn from me; for I am gentle and lowly in heart; and you will find rest for your souls. For my yoke is easy, and my burden is light."

I realized that for the past few months I had been trying to find happiness through worldly things, when all I needed was God. God knew what was best for me and was trying to show me that he is the joy in my life.

I turned my life over to God and really just let him work through me. I told my friends that I was discerning the priesthood, and it turned out that one of them was discerning a calling as well. We were able to talk about what we were going through together and pray together.

I was still apprehensive about making the decision between a college seminary and a regular university. I was praying hard about the whole situation, just looking for answers. I wanted to know right then whether or not I was supposed to be a priest. I remember praying for guidance at a prayer meeting one night, when I felt the presence of the Holy Spirit within me and heard him say simply, "Trust me; I won't mislead you."

From that point on I have been able to let God lead my life and trust that he knows what's best for me. I don't have to know God's entire plan. I trust that he is watching over me all the time and guiding me step by step.

I am living in the power of the Spirit, and it is just amazing the things he is doing in me and through me. I have found so much more joy in doing God's will than I ever had when I was living for myself.

Content With Myself

—Beth from Michigan, age eighteen

For years, every time I looked in the mirror or saw photos or videos of myself, I would cringe. I couldn't bear to look at my physical features. I tried to hide the ugliness I saw. I wore baggy clothes and hid my face under tons of makeup.

After a while, though, I gave up. I simply didn't care what I wore or how I appeared to other people. I convinced myself that no one saw me as an attractive woman of God. Oftentimes I found myself getting mad at God, asking him why he gave me my body.

As I went through middle school and high school, I became jealous of other girls who could wear anything and didn't need to try very hard to look good and attract guys. I never had a real boyfriend, and until recently I thought it was because I wasn't pretty enough.

I was sure that I could find true love only by having a boyfriend. In an attempt to find love, I turned to the sins of lust and gluttony. I thought that I had given my whole heart to God and that I had a relationship with him, but I was definitely wrong.

I attended youth group meetings during my four years of high school. I went through all the motions of serving and growing in community with my Catholic brothers and sisters. But I didn't really put my heart into it. I rarely prayed or even thought about God, even though I was at church all the time.

It wasn't until my senior year that I became tired of looking for "true love" by chasing after guys. I remember praying one day, "Please give me this love that I want. Please put something in my life that will give me this love."

Over the next few months, as a result of prayer, I began to realize the true meaning of love. An immense peace came over me, and I learned to be content with myself. I realized that God is love, the love I had been searching for in all the wrong places. God had been tapping me lightly on the shoulder and holding his arms out to me. I have come to realize that I am truly beautiful. God is in love with me, and he loves everything about me.

I battle Satan, who still tries to lure me into thinking that I can find "true love" through other things. While I am not perfect, I am trying to never take my eyes off the Love with which I have been captured. I have found God showing his love to me through very simple things—a butterfly, kids laughing, a sunset and the stars at night. Through these things I can hear the Lord whispering that he loves me.

Three Hours Seemed Like Ten Minutes
—Neil from Michigan, age twenty

During the fall of my senior year of high school, I was interested in devotion to God, but I was not devoted. I was free of grave sin through the fear of hell, but I still did not really love God. I was lukewarm.

God was about to wake me up. Even though I was spiritually lazy, God kept calling me until one experience of his devotion would not allow me to hold myself back from him any longer.

I was at eucharistic adoration with about a hundred other high school students on a youth retreat. At the beginning of this time there was charismatic worship, and I was very anxious. Many questions filled my mind as I was praying. Where am I going to college? What am I going to do with my life? Should I become a priest? I *want* to go to the University of Michigan; does that mean it's God's will? Why can't I just give my life to God? Do I even believe in him? Why can't I speak in tongues?

At that point I just gave up. The anxiety was too much for me. As I was kneeling there, I bent over and put my head on the ground, and then I went limp. I cleared my mind and heart, and I simply knelt in this position for a few minutes. When I collected myself, I said a simple prayer: "God if you want to show me something, then do it."

Suddenly I experienced a huge wave of joy, the kind of joy you can't explain in words. As I looked up at Jesus in the Blessed Sacrament, I had a mental image of truly kneeling at the foot of the cross on Calvary. I saw Jesus gazing down into my eyes from the cross, his blood running down to where I was on the ground. I then had the most profound experience of love. At this point I truly realized that Jesus *loves* me, that he burns with desire for me.

My catechism knowledge of God's love was converted to an understanding of God's love that can come only from a profound experience of it. I realized that all my anxieties are a waste of time because I love Jesus. Every flesh-centered, sinful, worldly endeavor is futile because Christ has conquered. I told Jesus then and there that he could have me.

That adoration time ended three hours later, but it seemed like ten minutes. The experience gave me such a grace of devotion that I have been able to make a holy hour every day for the past three years. Most of the time I do not feel the extraordinary graces in prayer that I did that day, yet prayer with God is truly the most satisfying thing that I do, because I am giving myself to my Creator.

A Fire in My Belly

—Daniel from Michigan, age eighteen

I was born into a Catholic family. Growing up I received the sacraments and went to Mass on Sundays. In fifth grade my class entered a speech contest about what we wanted to be when we grew up, and I said I wanted to be a priest. But I never realized the treasure God was giving me in the church.

As I entered high school, I lost track of my identity as a son of Christ and fell into the belief that the purpose of life was to do whatever I wanted. I got into the partying scene at school, though I found nothing there but depression and more anxiety. During my junior year, after a few events at a party, I realized that I needed to return to the Lord. Thankfully he took me back.

As the summer before my senior year drew to a close, a few friends invited me to a prayer meeting. I was not familiar with the Holy Spirit at all. I had heard people speak in tongues once, but I had no idea what it was; it just sounded cool.

During the prayer meeting one of my friends talked about the gift of tongues and how great it was to be able to pray in the Spirit. I asked my friends to pray over me. That day I was baptized in the Spirit and received the gift of tongues.

I used the gift of tongues occasionally, but it was not until our senior retreat that I first tried it out as I prayed over people. During the time of prayer with our small groups, everyone said very basic prayers, but I sensed that God wanted more, much more. We began to pray over each other, and I used the gift of tongues. The more I used it, the more I had a feeling of a fire in my belly. I just wanted to burst with praise to the Lord.

After the prayer groups we had a reconciliation service, and I felt that call coming back. God wanted me to surrender my life to him. I realized how weak I am without him and how much I had been trying to resist the call. I finally gave in and surrendered my life to Christ.

At that moment it felt as if a ton of bricks were being lifted off my back. I felt an overwhelming sense of peace and joy. This was true happiness, found only in the Lord. I went to confession, and the priest just happened to be the director of seminarians for the diocese. I told him about everything. He later helped me in the process of entering a college seminary.

After receiving reconciliation I went back into the chapel to pray. Two of my friends were there, and they asked if I wanted prayer. I couldn't refuse. As they prayed over me, I felt that fire growing in my belly. At one point I became so weak that I fell over. My emotions were bursting. I was crying and laughing, and I felt absolutely amazing. The entire experience was so incredible and real.

Since that night I have continued to use my gifts and have always found them to be a great, necessary help in overcoming obstacles. I have realized the importance of having the Holy Spirit present in my life, and I can truly say that Jesus Christ is Lord of my life.

Prompted by the Spirit
—*Peter from Michigan, age eighteen*

I grew up in a charismatic parish, with encouraging and devoted parents, and as a result I knew who the Holy Spirit was and had experienced his power. I learned at a young age to turn to the Lord, and I had heard his voice, but I had never been asked to do something specific. I loved God and his Spirit, but I was not ready to hear God's word and act on his order.

The summer after my ninth grade year, I served at a Christian boys' camp. Each day at camp we had an intense prayer time, and I could feel myself drawing closer and closer to the heart of God. More specifically, I was having a deeper awareness of the movement of the Holy Spirit.

In the middle of the week, we had an awesome prayer meeting. By this point many of the campers had experienced God and were giving themselves to him. However, there was one boy who hadn't participated at all during the daily prayer times, and the prayer meeting was no exception. He just sat in his seat and discouraged anyone from talking to him.

This boy was an acquaintance, and I knew that he had a tough life, but I did not feel qualified to reach him. As I was looking at him and quietly praying for him, I clearly heard the Lord tell me to go and talk to him and tell him how much he was loved. My initial reaction was, "No way, God; ask someone else." But the Spirit of God was tugging strongly on my heart, and I started to give in.

I asked God for more love, because my embarrassment and fear were overshadowing the love I had for the boy. The Lord then sent his Spirit into my heart, and I saw everyone in the room with a small piece of the love that God had for each one. I started crying, and I knew that I wouldn't survive unless I talked to the boy.

I went over to him and asked him if I could talk to him. He reluctantly agreed, and we went to the back of the room. There I proceeded to pour out to him how much he was loved and how much God desired his heart. I had a hard time talking because the tears were still flowing, but I felt that the Holy Spirit was directing my words. After about five minutes I looked over and saw that the boy was crying as well.

At this point one of the counselors took over, and I went back to praying with the other campers. I felt an incredible sense of God's pride and satisfaction because I had done his will. That night the boy gave his life to Jesus, and I felt so blessed that the Holy Spirit had used me to build the kingdom.

I still struggle with acting on the promptings of the Holy Spirit, but he continues to remind me of the good that happens when I follow his lead.

Extreme Protection and Peace
—David from Michigan, age eighteen

I was raised a Catholic. I was baptized, received my first Communion, went to confession and was confirmed, but I didn't know the true significance of these sacraments in my life. In late middle school and early high school, I realized that I didn't know very much about the person of Jesus, and I definitely didn't know who the Holy Spirit was.

Before my freshman year of high school, my family and I moved and changed parishes. Our new parish was very charismatic, and the people there were on fire for Jesus and the Holy Spirit. I always had tried to live by correct morals, but it seemed as if these people had more than that: They had a connection with God and the Holy Spirit that I had never experienced.

During my senior year I attended a Life in the Spirit Seminar and received the gift of tongues, but I didn't use it much after that. I simply received the gift and let it sit inside me.

On my senior retreat the time came for me to take a step toward God. I had a friend who had just found God on the retreat. He stepped forward and said with tears in his eyes that he wanted to pray out loud for each person in our small group. It was clear that he was not accustomed to praying aloud, and his words were awkward. It was at this moment that I sensed the Holy Spirit at work in me.

The Spirit was tugging on my heart to pray for my friend. I felt a warm and tingly sensation on my neck and upper back. I was afraid, but I extended my hand and began praying out loud to God, imploring him to help my friend, to guide his thoughts and words so that the person he was praying over would be touched.

Almost immediately my friend began saying beautiful things about each individual in the room. The tingling sensation inside of me turned to fire and moved up to my face and down to my feet. I felt extreme protection and peace. Eventually I stopped using words and began to pray in the Spirit, letting One much greater than I ask God for guidance for my friend.

I could tell that the words of my friend were touching others. He was expressing all his true feelings for each person from the depths of his heart, and tears streamed down his face and my own. I was so glad that the Holy Spirit could use me as an instrument to help others in their walk of faith while deepening my own walk of faith.

God Makes a Way

—*Mike from New Hampshire, young adult*

In early September 2004 I decided to make Ste. Marie's my parish. At the end of a Mass, there was an announcement about the formation of a young adult ministry. This was too good to be true. I had been looking for something in the church that would address the needs of someone my age. I was just out of college, unmarried and not sure where God was leading. I immediately put my name on the list, and though I was the only one from my family there at the time, I added my brothers' names as well.

The first meeting was in December at the rectory. There were about twenty of us there. During the meeting it became apparent to me that this was a place where I would find other young adults who were trying to live as Catholics.

Toward the end of the meeting, everyone agreed we should meet regularly. We discussed what would be the best day and time for the majority of people. I explained, "The only evening I cannot come is Tuesday, because I have classes from 6:00 to 9:00 PM." Unfortunately, Tuesday from 8:00 to 9:00 was the time the majority of people could make it.

I thought God had directed me to be a part of this group, and now I would not be able to attend any of their meetings. I had been so excited about the group. I went home that night more than a little disappointed.

I sought my parents for some insight. They too felt that God had been calling me to be a member of this young adult group. They told me to be patient, because if God wanted me to be a part of the group, he would open doors for me. That night I prayed and tried to give it all to God.

The next meeting was cancelled because of a heavy snowfall. To my surprise and disappointment, my class was not cancelled.

This was the first class of the new semester, and the room was packed. The instructor announced that since there were so many students in the class, he was going to try to open another section on Thursday if enough people signed up. I thought, "I don't want to give up my Thursday evenings to be in class." So when the sign-up sheet went around the first time, I did not sign up.

During the class, as I was listening and taking notes, I remembered that the young adult meetings were on Tuesday evenings. If I signed up for the Thursday class, I would not miss the meetings. The next time the sign-up sheet came around, I signed it.

Needless to say, the professor received permission to open up the new section, and I was able to attend the young adult meetings. Since I joined the group my life has changed substantially. I have learned that I am not alone in my thirst for God and that I can live a joyful life as I continue my quest for a deeper relationship with him.

Delivered From Evil

—Theresia from Germany, age twenty-three

I had a personal encounter with Jesus in 1997, but I was still searching for his love for me. I believed in God, I experienced his work in my life, I felt the love he had for me and I heard fascinating stories of what God had done in people's lives. I wanted to believe in him, but I had a persisting doubt about his existence.

This was a difficult time for me. It seemed as if the more I wanted to know God's love, the more the doubt in me was growing. I hated myself for this doubt. I confessed it and tried all I could to rid myself of it, but it was still there.

In 2005, after graduating from college, I took six months off to spend time focusing on God. I attended a missions school in India, expecting God to change something in my life. And he did.

We had several lessons on the power of the Holy Spirit, on spiritual warfare and on God's love and plan for our lives. During this time it became clear to me that this doubt couldn't be God's will for me.

I received prayer for the baptism in the Holy Spirit. I had pain in me, and I just cried to know the love of God. All I wanted was to be loved, but for some reason I couldn't feel it. Then, at the end of the prayer session, I received tremendous joy from God. I couldn't stop laughing for an hour. This was amazing! I never had felt so much joy.

The next few days we spoke about spiritual warfare. I felt crushed again, the joy was gone and doubt was back. We had a few ministry times during those days, when we prayed especially to know God's love. I just felt pain. Everybody around me was filled with the Holy Spirit, and I had nothing. The doubts about God were worse than before. I kept thinking, "God isn't real. I should go home. Nothing will ever change!"

In reality I wanted nothing more than to be near God's heart, to know with every part of my body and soul that he is real. This was why I didn't give up, even though I knew that I didn't have the power anymore to fight.

At the end of the week I had a special prayer time with the two guest speakers. For some reason this felt like my last chance, and something inside of me tried to keep me away from it. Thanks be to God that my will won this fight.

The result of this prayer time was the deliverance of a demon. I could physically feel the power of the Holy Spirit at work inside of me. The demon left, and the Holy Spirit came to fill me with the Father's amazing love. I felt God sitting beside me, hugging me. I felt him stroke my face. This was the first time in my life I felt loved by God without doubting it, the first time I was sure that I was loved.

This new certainty changed me completely. It set me free to become the woman God wants me to be. I do not have to hide anymore. I now can go to people I do not know and speak with them because I know that God loves me.

I am so thankful that God and the Holy Spirit never gave up on me. I am very sure that it was the Holy Spirit who never let me give up, who gave me the strength to believe in God when everything inside of me screamed, "No!" It was the Holy Spirit who let this desire grow, the desire to know God and know his love.

CHAPTER THREE

Promptings of the Spirit in Ordinary Life

I am with you always.

Matthew 28:20

My Priorities Needed Adjusting

—Tim from Michigan

Over the years I have been blessed to see the Holy Spirit work in power with manifestations of signs and wonders. I have seen people healed physically and set free from significant oppression by the Evil One. I have seen the Spirit reveal hidden things about people through words of knowledge and prophecy, so that they can enter more fully into the Lord's love, grace and power. Sometimes the Lord has even used *me* as the human instrument through which he accomplishes these works!

It always is exhilarating and exciting to see these things and to be used by the Lord in this way. Sadly, for a long time I evaluated my fruitfulness for the Lord with undue emphasis on these spiritual gifts.

But I have come to realize that if I am attentive, the Holy Spirit will guide me into an even greater manifestation of God's power: a transformation of my selfish nature through the virtue of charity. As with most of my stumbling steps forward on the path of holiness, my wife played a leading role in this realization.

My lovely bride of many years is a high-energy servant. She is constantly involved in some type of parental oversight or other work that needs to be done to make our household run smoothly. She is worn out by bedtime, and sometimes it can take her a long time to unwind.

I, on the other hand, fall asleep within seconds of my head hitting the pillow. At times she would ask within this interval for a back rub to help her relax so she could fall asleep. Despite her hard work all day, I would grumble and complain. Either I would agree reluctantly to do it, or I would refuse because I was too tired.

On one occasion when I was giving her a reluctant back rub, I turned to the Lord and offered it up to him. As I did so, I sensed the Holy Spirit convicting me of my selfishness and failure to love. I was reminded of 1 Corinthians 13 and the superiority of charity over other spiritual gifts. I placed a lot of emphasis on following the leading of the Spirit in prayer and ministry to people, but did I look to the Spirit to guide me in the way of charity? My priorities needed to be adjusted.

Since that day I have tried to comply with my wife's requests for a backrub. Sometimes I anticipate her needs and offer even before she asks. I have tried to do it quietly, without bringing attention to what I am doing. I've tried also to look for more ways to quietly show charity to her.

Now that the secret is out, I will need to look for additional ways to show my wife charity. It's not quite heroic virtue, I know, but for me it is a good start! *Come, Holy Spirit, and guide me into the way of love!*

Granola Crumbs and Answered Prayer
—*Debbie Herbeck*

A week before leaving for Mexico to lead a mission trip for high school students, I was looking frantically for my passport. Just a month earlier I had returned from a medical mission trip in Nicaragua, and I thought I had put my passport in a safe place, knowing that I would need it again soon. But after looking unsuccessfully in all the most likely places, including my suitcase, I finally turned to the Lord for help.

On Monday morning I went to my Bible study leaders' meeting and asked several women to pray that my passport would show up. The specific prayer of one woman impressed me: "O Lord, help Debbie find her passport quickly. If it's in a hidden place, make its location really obvious to her."

I returned home later in the day, about a half hour after my kids had come home from school. I was tired and a bit annoyed to see my eleven-year-old daughter's backpack sitting on the dining room table, in the middle of a large pile of crumbs from a crushed granola bar. I picked up her backpack and shook the crumbs off, and out fell my passport!

I had forgotten that I had borrowed my daughter's backpack on my last trip and had left my passport there in a hidden pocket. The crushed granola bar was my mess, left over from the trip!

Not only did the Holy Spirit answer that very specific prayer, but also I learned an important lesson about experiencing God's provision, even in the "messiness" of life.

Soy Sauce and the Nudge of the Spirit

—*Donna from Toronto, Canada*

One evening, my hands full with preparing dinner and helping the children with their homework, I consistently felt the nudge to clean out my pantry. I initially resisted the idea because I was busy enough as it was, but that sense of insistence to clean out the pantry right away would not stop. So I yielded and began emptying the shelves.

To my surprise I discovered that I had two unopened bottles of soy sauce. My first thought was to call my friend and neighbor Mariette, whose husband was without work and whose family was suffering financially. I explained to her that I had this relentless urge to clean out my pantry and discovered these two bottles. I asked her if she wanted one.

There was a long silence, and I could hear Mariette crying softly. I asked her what was wrong, and through her tears she recounted how she had been standing over the stove thinking how nice it would be to have soy sauce to go with the pork chops she was preparing for dinner. We both were touched by the tender love of our awesome God, who had heard Mariette and responded to her desire for this small item.

Safe in God's Arms
—Steve from Iowa

It will be seven years this July that my younger sister died. Mary had always been active in her Catholic faith, finding time to share the holy Eucharist with patients in a nearby hospital as well as being active and available to serve in her local parish.

Mary had suffered from childhood of severe diabetes. She had been through several transplants, one for a kidney and later a pancreas. The doctors agreed that she was one of the country's longest living dual transplant recipients.

It was in March of 2000 that Mary was diagnosed with an aggressive, inoperable brain cancer. She was not given much hope for life, and because she was growing progressively weaker, she elected not to seek further medical treatment. It was decided that she would return home and receive hospice care.

On a Sunday afternoon in March my wife and I went to visit Mary and her family. I remember this particular afternoon as being quite tedious. It had been several hours since either of us had eaten. It was our plan to leave the house for a while, grab a bite to eat and maybe return later in the evening.

As it turned out, we felt the Holy Spirit telling us to remain at the house with Mary. Several hours later she developed some very shallow breathing, and she died with us and other family members gathered at her bedside to weep and say some final prayers. Many of us in the room experienced a sense of peace and of spiritual well-being that I cannot describe. It was as if God was saying to us, "Do not fear; she is now safe in my arms."

Warmed by God's Love

—Deanna from Michigan

When our family lived in Minneapolis, I saw in a store one day a beautiful, 100-percent wool sweater, size medium, for $6.40. I immediately thought of John R., a good friend who had lived with us for two years and had worked at one time with my husband. John didn't have a lot of money because he had taken a job that allowed him time to work with the Hmong, the mountain people of Vietnam, many of whom relocated to Minneapolis after the war.

I bought the sweater for John and wrapped it up, although it wasn't his birthday. I had never given him a gift before, nor have I since. Bill, a neighbor who worked with John, stopped by that evening and took the present to give to John the next day.

John stopped by the next day to tell me the beautiful way God had blessed him. Earlier that week he had been with a Hmong friend at his apartment. It was very cold, and he decided to give his friend his favorite sweater, which was heavy and warm. The very next day he went to work and received a new wool sweater!

Praise God for his faithfulness to his children! For me this was a confirmation that God is speaking to me and that I am able to hear and respond to him.

An Unexpected Return to the Church

—*Tom from New York*

I was baptized Catholic, but my parents divorced when I was young, and they never followed through with any further religious education for my brother or me. I tried getting involved with a Catholic church when I was in the Air Force, but I was going for the wrong reason—trying to meet girls—and never truly understood the meaning of the Mass.

After a couple of years I no longer went to church, except for a funeral or wedding. I never had any thoughts or desires to learn more about the faith. I also started to lead a very sinful life. I was running an illegal business, and all my thoughts and actions revolved around making money. I was also having sexual relations with many women.

When it came to getting married, I would not have the ceremony in the church, even with my wife's insistence. I stubbornly refused to go through the RCIA classes to complete the sacraments I had not received as a child. I had nothing against the church; I just did not want anyone telling me what to do.

After six years of marriage we had a beautiful baby girl. She was baptized Catholic, and we planned to raise her Catholic. This still had no effect on my relationship with the church.

One day I was out shopping with my brother-in-law. I decided to wait in the car with my sleeping daughter while he ran into a store. An announcement came over the radio that our Holy Father Pope John Paul II had passed away. This brought tears to my eyes, and suddenly I felt I had to return to the church. I could not explain this; it came out of nowhere and hit me like a ton of bricks. I knew the church was where I belonged. I immediately enrolled in the next RCIA class at our parish.

I feel truly touched by the Holy Spirit. For the first time in my life I have a peace that I have never known. I wish our RCIA classes were more than once a week—I can't get enough! I read as much as I can to learn about our faith. I have recently discovered

Catholic radio, which helps me keep our Lord in my thoughts throughout each day.

I look forward to making my First Communion and confirmation at the Easter Vigil. I thank and praise God every day for calling me home to this wonderful church and for all of the blessings he has given me my whole life, even when I turned my back on him.

No Matter What
—*Deacon Bob from Michigan*

In January of 1976 my wife and I were introduced to the Catholic charismatic renewal at a little prayer meeting in our local parish. What I encountered in those meetings stirred me to the core. I was both attracted to things wonderful and repulsed by things strange. Sensing the Spirit of God at close range, my heart had little strength, and I struggled to know how to pray.

By April a powerful question began to repeat itself in my mind: "Will you give your whole life to me, no matter what?" I felt that this question was coming right from God, and it thoroughly sobered me. Indeed, nothing had ever induced more fear in me than this bold question. It was the "no matter what" phrase that sent me reeling. I said no to this question every day and many times each day from April through the middle of August.

In August we went to my in-laws' lakefront cottage with the family. One morning right after dawn, before the commotion of the day began, I went out alone to swim. The water was like glass. I stood facing the shore, water up to my neck, and prayed about the same—now exhausting—question that had taken up permanent residence in me.

Suddenly from the tip of my toes to the top of my head, a great surging "Yes!" welled up in me. I shouted out, "Yes, the answer to your question is yes!" It was the most wholehearted moment of my life. Yet this wide-open response was not of my own making. I could tell that it had come from far away.

A few weeks later at the same lakefront cottage, I went to bed early after a vigorous day in the sun with our five kids, aged two through nine. It was the Sunday evening before Labor Day, September 5, 1976. I couldn't have been in bed more than ten minutes when I was suddenly immersed in an experience that would change my life. The nature and intensity of what happened that evening defied words, but every cell in my body knew instantly how to name it. This was Jesus!

The love of Jesus came over me completely. Lying on the bed, I was utterly overwhelmed. The sensation was that of being fully, unbelievably loved. His love found its mark, perfectly matching every true need in me. I cried so hard; these were tears of pure joy—the joy of a lifetime, the joy of unqualified love, the joy of him!

I do not know how long my experience of the Lord's love continued, but I'd guess that it was in the range of one to five minutes. And then he spoke to me, deep within. I didn't see or hear anything in the normal ways of perception, but he spoke a totally surprising message right into my heart. He said, "You have struggled with openness to life. Now that struggle is over with, and it will be OK."

I hadn't been thinking seriously about "that matter" for many months, but apparently he had. The matter in question (and my heart knew exactly what he meant) was that of contraception.

Two years earlier I had become intimidated by our burgeoning family size, since I was the sole wage earner with a fairly modest employment as a research engineer at the University of Michigan. My wife and I really loved all these kids; we cherished them. But an inordinate concern over my family responsibilities had caused me to argue for a contraceptive practice right after the birth of our fifth child. We sought pastoral advice before taking this step, but it was a confused time, and my heart was eager to take soft guidance.

When the Lord's merciful message came to me on that September evening, all confusion and resistance vanished. His light was shining into my darkness, and there was no overcoming it.

After receiving this message, the experience ended. The momentous event of his love was an historical marker that signaled the close of the first major stage of my life. My whole sense of reality had turned as on a hinge when Jesus' love was revealed to me.

Late in the next year we had our sixth child, a daughter. We were jubilant at her arrival. She grew up to be a lovely woman, and at this writing she's about to be married. Eighteen months after our daughter's birth, our son was born. He became a mechanical engineer, and he's a prince of a young man before God.

These two young people might not have been. Although we have the same unbounded love for all seven of our kids, the last two are undeniably the children of God's vigorous mercy. His mercy won out over our small-hearted fears.

Stocking Up

—Simone from Austria

The first time I visited the United States, I was part of the big blackout all along the East Coast and as far west as Michigan.

Earlier in the day I was running errands with a friend, driving around from place to place. Although I was tired and eager to get back to the place where I was staying, I felt the Holy Spirit calling my name. I suddenly had this amazing urge to go shopping and to buy specific items: candles, batteries and water.

As I couldn't resist this urge, we went to a store to buy those items. When I came home I still didn't understand why I had to buy those things in particular, but three hours later, when all the electricity went out, I knew.

Pleased That You Are Here

—Jeanette from Michigan

Going to eucharistic adoration weekly, I became familiar with the regular attendees. One day, as often happens, someone new entered to worship. This unfamiliar person quietly and reverently took a seat in the pew in front of me. As she did, I heard a voice from within me say: "Ask me what I'd say to her, if I were going to say something."

I asked the Lord, "What would you say?" Much to my surprise I heard: "I would tell her how pleased I am that she is here." I thought to myself, "How nice," and turned back to my own prayer.

After a while I felt the Lord wanted me to communicate his thoughts to her. So, finding a piece of paper and a pencil, I wrote: "The Lord wants you to know how pleased he is that you are here." I tapped her on the shoulder and laid the note beside her. I returned to prayer and forgot the incident.

A few weeks later, at a parish prayer meeting, a woman approached me. She asked, "Do you remember me?" I didn't. She informed me that she was the woman in the chapel that day. She said that she had struggled with whether or not the Lord was truly calling her to adore him in the Eucharist.

"Now," she said, "there can be no doubt. The confirmation has come through a total stranger."

Cutting Through Red Tape
—*Bernice from Ghana, Africa*

My husband and I are leaders of an international lay movement in Ghana. We were invited, along with two of our staff members, to Ireland to help with a leadership course that was scheduled to begin on May 11. Knowing the difficulty involved in visa situations in Africa, we made sure we provided all the required information, and we prayed over all our applications before sending them.

Two weeks after the program had started, we still had not heard from the consular's office. All efforts by our host to get the visa office to monitor the visa process had proved futile. It was at this point that I felt the Holy Spirit leading our team to declare three days of prayer and fasting, in addition to praying the Divine Mercy Chaplet for the situation.

On the very first day of the fast, from our host came a message that our applications had been located. The visa office said it would take three more weeks before a decision could be made. We were disturbed because we knew the program would be over in the next four weeks. However, we were encouraged when the Holy Spirit directed us to the Scripture passage that says that a thousand years are like a day before God (see 2 Peter 3:8).

On the second day of the fast, on my way to evening Mass, I passed by an Internet café to check my e-mail. Our host had e-mailed to say that the visa office now planned to make the decision in two to three days instead of three weeks. And then the greatest miracle happened: We found out on the third day of the fast that our visa had been granted.

We obtained our visas and made it to the program. We had a blessed time. Indeed, we have a great God who has authority over everything. Thank you, Holy Spirit, for your direction!

Another Ed

—Ed from Indiana

Approximately ten years ago I was going through a very tough time in my life. I spent most mornings walking two or three miles. I had returned only recently to the Catholic church after several years away, and I was still trying to sort out many aspects of my life. One morning I asked God to provide me with a sign that he really did exist and that he cared for me.

I work with teens on retreats called Teens Encounter Christ. There was a gentleman who always cleaned the buildings after the retreats. His name, like mine, was Ed. He had been sick for a while, and the Lord took him home one day. The thought came to me that maybe if I asked the right person, I could take his place.

I saw a good friend named Linda, who did a lot at these retreats, and I asked her if I could take Ed's place as the clean-up guy. She and a woman she was sitting with looked at each other in a funny way, and Linda said, "Yes, you can."

At the next retreat Linda told me the real story. She and Ed had been very good friends, and she was with him right before he passed away. Linda told him to please send her another Ed to be like the angel he was.

A Bouquet, a Bulletin and Baptism
—*Elaine from Michigan*

My husband and I were invited to have dinner with an Egyptian family who lived in a small family apartment on the campus of a nearby university. Their little boy needed physical therapy every week, and I had helped them by driving him to the appointments.

After dinner we went outside to their picnic table to have dessert. I happened to glance next door, and there was an Asian grandmother holding a new baby. She smiled at us, and it was obvious that she wanted us to see this newborn. I walked over to her and asked how old the baby was. The grandmother said, "Iris."

She could not speak any English, but soon the baby's parents came outside. I introduced myself and told them their baby was beautiful, just like the beautiful flower also named iris. They hurried back inside to get their dictionary and look up the word *iris*. I soon went back to visit with our friends.

The next morning we were getting ready to take a vacation with our entire family. Iris and her family continued to come to my mind, however, and I had a strong urge from the Holy Spirit to go buy a bouquet of iris and take it to this family I had met the night before. My husband said, "Are you sure? Then I will take you so you don't spill the water all over the car."

After two stops I found the perfect flowers. Then we drove to our church, which is near the family's apartment, and picked up a church bulletin for the services the following day. We drove to the apartment, and the family greeted me with smiles and many thanks when I knocked on their door.

When we came back from our vacation two weeks later, there was a thank-you note in our mailbox at church. They have been attending our church each week since then and would like to be baptized soon.

Thank you, Holy Spirit, for those quiet nudges you give us.

A Little Too Comfortable

—*Cecile from Minnesota*

I was born and raised Catholic. I attended Catholic grade school and high school and also a Catholic college for one year. I've always had a strong faith and in recent years a devotion to the Holy Spirit. I have been praying a novena to the Holy Spirit quite regularly.

Both my husband and I are now retired and have a good life. I do some volunteer work, belong to a ladies' church group, help with church and community events and have traveled quite a bit with my husband.

One day it occurred to me that my life was at a stage where it had become very comfortable—for which I am grateful to God—but maybe just a little too comfortable. I think the Holy Spirit was calling me to do a little something more. So last year when a course came to our parish on how to evangelize people, I knew this was something I needed to try.

I am now taking this course for the second time and have become quite involved with it. I am a shy person, and the Holy Spirit has helped me to open up and meet and become friends with other good Christian people.

I am also taking some classes to learn more about Jesus and to find out what God's purpose is for me. I am reading the Bible daily. I am excited to know God's purpose for me and to continue doing God's work in spreading his word to others.

God Pays the Rent

—Lloyd from Florida

Fifteen years ago my wife Nancy and I felt God's call to serve the Catholic church full-time as missionary evangelists. After much prayer and spiritual direction from our pastor, we decided to step out in faith and trust God for the results. We told God that if he made the appointments, we would keep them.

When we started out, the greatest struggle for me was in the area of finances. I had worked for over twenty-five years as a manufacturer's representative for several large companies and had always made good money. Now I knew that, without a Roman collar around my neck, it would be difficult to get paid for preaching the Good News. We tried several things on the side to "help God out" with providing for us, but nothing seemed to work. Nancy and I came before the Lord, and he told us, "Trust me; I will be your provider."

We decided that the Lord wanted us not to charge for the youth retreats, parish missions and days of renewal we were holding but rather to rely on him alone. We sensed that this approach would be a way for us to discern what God was asking us to do. If we felt the Lord wanted us to go to Cuba, provision of the money would mean it was his will. If no money came in, the answer was no.

The first years were the hardest; there was a lot of testing. We learned firsthand the value of asking God to "give us this day our daily bread." Our faith was strong enough for that day. We lived by faith from day to day.

The beauty of this type of life was that we had proof that God will provide, and each day, each trip to another state or country, reinforced God's promise to us. After fifteen years we have many testimonies showing that God is never outdone in generosity and that we can put our trust in him.

Although we did not have any training in writing, we felt that the Lord wanted us to start a monthly newsletter to let people know what God was doing around the world through ordinary people like us. Every time we did a retreat or mission, we put out a sign-up sheet, and our reader base slowly grew. We started to include a tithe envelope in the newsletter to allow people to participate in our missionary work.

At the end of one month we were forced to make a decision. The $600 rent on our house was due, and it was time to mail the newsletter. At that time it cost $385 to send out the newsletter, and we had $400 in the bank. Should we pay the rent or send out the newsletter?

It was not an easy decision. After much prayer and soul-searching, we decided that God wanted us to use the newsletter as part of our teaching ministry, and in faith we sent it out. The next day I went to our post office box and found several tithe envelopes, some junk mail and what I thought was a carnival advertisement from a local Presbyterian church. I thanked God for the few checks that had come in, but they were far less than what we needed.

For some reason I opened the envelope from the Presbyterian church. In it was a check for $800! This church had been given a large sum of money for the work of evangelization, and each year they gave the interest from this money to a worthwhile organization. I later found out that someone who had come to our prayer meeting from that church had been touched by the Lord and had recommended us to the church council as a candidate for the money.

One morning it was again rent time. There was no money in the bank, and we needed the $600 that day. My faith was low, and I had no idea what we should do to get the money. Nancy said, "Don't worry; God will provide."

Around two o'clock we received a phone call from a woman for whom we had prayed a few months earlier. God had healed her of the depression she had had for fourteen years, and the change in her life and family was dramatic! Her atheist husband was so moved by her transformation that he accepted Jesus as his Savior, and that Easter he became Catholic.

This couple had recently come into some money. They now felt that God wanted them to share some of it with us. They gave us a check for $600, the exact amount of our rent!

Two Raffle Tickets
—Nicole from Michigan

Jesus said to his disciples: "Ask, and it will be given you; seek, and you will find; knock, and it will be opened to you. For every one who asks receives, and he who seeks finds, and to him who knocks it will be opened" (Matthew 7:7–8).

I was listening to this Gospel reading at Mass at my parents' church one Sunday in July. I had been praying about my financial situation for months. The reading confirmed that I needed to keep praying. So I did some serious soul-searching that Sunday morning. I asked. I sought. I knocked.

I was working as a youth and young adult minister and just loved my job. I loved sharing my faith with others. I loved the parish where I worked. I loved seeing how our Lord would work and move in the hearts of the youth and young adults. I really felt that this was where our Lord had called me to serve. But my salary was not paying the bills.

It seemed that the Lord was asking me to trust him with my finances. This is one of those areas of my life where I play tug-of-war with our Lord. I trust, I let go, but then I start to worry again.

I really talked to God after Communion that day, not holding anything back. "Lord, how am I supposed to pay my bills? Should I look for another job? Where do you want me to be, Lord? My car is dying, my debts are adding up, and it really is stressing me out!" I thought of Mother Teresa and how she totally trusted that our Lord would provide for her needs and the needs of those she served.

After Mass the parish was having its annual picnic. There was a raffle in conjunction with the picnic. The proceeds would go to the college scholarship fund, and since I had received two scholarships from the parish, I bought two tickets.

It was a beautiful day for a picnic, and I had a great time visiting with family and friends. Then came the drawing for the raffle. There were several winners that day, but the big ticket was mine! In total shock, I started shaking! I had just won $20,000!

Our Lord knows our needs and takes care of every one, though maybe not all our wants. Twenty thousand dollars is *a lot* of money, but it was just what I needed to pay off my debts so that I could continue serving the church. When we ask, seek and knock, we can trust that our Lord will open the door that needs to be opened.

Flowers From God's Heart
—*Michelle from Michigan*

It was a warm Friday in June, and my five daughters were piled into our tightly packed minivan. My husband was out of town, and the rest of us were heading to Ohio to visit relatives. We had been scrambling since sunup to pack our things and get out the door.

When I at last turned on the porch light and locked the front door, I hesitated on the steps. We were already two hours past our scheduled departure time. But all morning my mind had been distracted by a strong impression that I should visit the grave of my friend's son, who had died at the age of twenty-one just a few months before. Not just visit either, but bring flowers from my garden to plant.

I can't go, I thought. *My mom is waiting for me three hours away; we have plans for the afternoon.*

I began to walk to the car, then stopped abruptly. No, I had to do it. I turned and ran around the back of the house to the garden shed.

When I reappeared twenty minutes later with a shovel, a hoe, a cultivator and paper sacks of freshly dug plants, the girls' faces registered disbelief and frustration. "I have to go to Tim's grave before we leave," I said. "It's the Holy Spirit; I have to listen."

We drove in silence, first to the nursery for a flat of bright impatiens, then to the quiet church cemetery. Some of the girls got out to help while I weeded, turned the soil and designed a semicircular flower bed where there had been weedy moss and hard-packed clay. We prayed for Tim's soul and for my friend Lorrie and her family. Finally we hit the road.

About a week later I was catching up on some business at my desk, and I reviewed the calendar. With disappointment I saw that I had missed Lorrie's birthday the Friday before. Then I realized that I hadn't missed it! Or rather, the Holy Spirit *in me* hadn't missed it.

I had that sudden awed wonder that comes when we realize that God sees and that we are not alone. Through his Holy Spirit he involves himself, even in small details, to show his love for us and through us to show his love for others.

Later I called Lorrie and found out that she had visited her son's grave that Friday afternoon of her birthday. The fresh plants had spoken to her heart about the truth of the Resurrection.

CHAPTER FOUR

Strength for Living

*Know that the Lord has set apart
the godly for himself;
the Lord hears when I call to him.*

Psalm 4:3

Another Child for Us

—Anilu from Michigan

After nine years of marriage, three children and four miscarriages, I wasn't sure I wanted to "try again." I had come from a family of seven and had always wanted to have a big family. My husband had come from a small family and had experienced loneliness growing up; he too wanted a big family. But we never anticipated the difficulties we would encounter. I had experienced God's love and mercy through it all, but at this point I felt spent.

Now the specialist's words were, "Go ahead and try again." But I wanted a guarantee that this time everything would be OK. I wanted to trust, but I couldn't. I remember my prayer: "Holy Spirit, guide us."

As I stood at the doctor's office crying, my husband hugged me and said, "I feel that the Lord has another child for us." My husband and I pray together every night, and I knew that I could trust his love for me, but more than that I could trust his desire to do God's will. There in that office, with no guarantee from the doctor but with the assurance of the Holy Spirit in our lives, I agreed to try again.

A few months later I found myself pregnant. Eight weeks into the pregnancy, as I watched my kids play on their swing set, I started to bleed profusely. I was scared and called my husband.

As we drove to the doctor's office, I remembered my husband's earlier sense that the Lord had a child for us. I said to the Lord, "I don't have what it takes to trust at this moment, but I know that your Holy Spirit inspired my husband. I believe that your Holy Spirit is active in our lives today. You need to guide the doctor now."

The baby was still alive, and I was put on bed rest for many weeks. Usually active and able to serve others, this time was hard for me. As the weeks went by, the Lord showed me that this was "my turn" to be on the stretcher and let my friends carry me up to the roof, then down to the feet of Jesus, as in the second chapter of Mark's Gospel. It was my friends' turn to have faith for me.

Every day and night over the next few months, I experienced the Holy Spirit bringing peace and order to what otherwise would be fear and turmoil as I continued to bleed off and on. With three little ones at home and being confined to bed, I knew it was not up to me. The Lord had to work everything out.

Our daughter was born strong and healthy on the Feast of the Presentation of the Lord. The Holy Spirit was upon Simeon; there are three different references to the Holy Spirit in that short passage of Luke 2:25. Just like Simeon, we blessed God for his faithfulness and for walking with us and teaching us how to wait on him throughout that previous year.

Breaking Through the Small Talk
—*Donna from Canada*

The theme of the prayer meeting was yet another new discovery for me, as we talked and prayed about how to avoid being lukewarm Christians. God wanted us to witness to his presence in our lives, and we were not to be hesitant to speak about him to others.

My initial reaction to this teaching was one of reluctance, and this I immediately brought before Jesus. I told him that I was not prepared to stand on a street corner proclaiming the gospel message. So I asked that, if he ever wanted me to speak about him to anyone, he would please make it *very clear.*

The next morning at work, I was on my way to get a drink from the water fountain when a colleague greeted me and made his way toward me. In the course of our small talk, he asked what I had done the previous night. My heart began racing as I realized that this was an opportunity the Lord was giving me to witness to him. Despite a momentary fear of being ridiculed, I could not dodge so direct a call to respond to God's message.

"I was at a Catholic charismatic prayer meeting," I said, to which he replied, "Wow, will you take me with you to the next one?"

Awestruck, I inquired if he was Catholic. He said yes. I told him he could join me the following Tuesday evening.

I praised God. I could not get over the beauty of what he had just allowed to happen. Then I began to ask Jesus how this man would respond to the prayer meeting and how I could prepare him for something he probably had never been exposed to. As I was pondering all this, the man appeared at my office door with a bouquet of flowers, thanking me for our conversation. I was speechless with joy.

Much later I found out that this young man was Catholic but only in name. At one time he had been involved with Hare Krishna. We went out that Saturday, and God was the focal point of our conversation and our evening.

The following day was Palm Sunday, and the Lord was beginning to enter this young man's life as dramatically as he had entered Jerusalem two thousand years ago. He felt a need to go back to Mass for the first time in more than fifteen years, and he found a church that offered a 5:00 PM Mass. There it was announced that confessions were scheduled for 7:00 PM that evening, so he returned to church later for that. Needless to say, he thoroughly enjoyed the prayer meeting the following Tuesday and felt completely at home.

We dated for two years and had countless adventures on our journey of spiritual growth. We were married in the month of May, the month dedicated to our heavenly Mother, on the eve of Pentecost in 1977, a holy year declared by our wonderful Pope John Paul II. We are in our twenty-eighth year of marriage with three children, and our love for God and one another continues to deepen and grow.

Out of the Depths
—Debra from Minnesota

I find it extremely difficult to put into words the transformation Jesus has accomplished in me. It's nothing short of miraculous. Jesus Christ is now the center of my life and my world.

Jesus, through the Holy Spirit, took me from the depths of despair to unspeakable joy. I was a person who never touched or hugged because I was unable to let people get close to the real me. On the outside, my life appeared to be together. I had a loving husband, children, a good job and a nice home. But the reality of my hidden life was that I felt totally unlovable and of no value to anyone. I lived in a shell and the walls I built for self-protection isolated me.

When I gave my life to Christ, my walls tumbled down. The name of Jesus had once made me uneasy, but now I long for the opportunity to talk about him and share with others his incredible love. Going to church, which had been a task, became an opportunity to express my love and to discover more about him. The Eucharist has so captured my heart that I became a eucharistic minister. As a way of expressing my gratitude and love for God, I helped start a program in our parish to assist people in need.

The more I give myself to Christ, the more I receive of His unchanging love, mercy and grace. It is such an honor to get up every day and pray and rejoice in the Lord.

My husband and daughter have both given their lives to Christ. We are able to share life together on a whole new level because of this. My husband and I have seen lives changed and we've witnessed God's healing power. We've participated in classes and led groups in the parish and have gone to many charismatic retreats and conferences as part of our annual vacation.

I am honored to know Jesus as my personal Savior. I know of his incredible mercy and I can't wait for each new day to walk hand in hand with my Lord.

Confronting Fear

—Michelle from Michigan

Since the age of eight or nine years, I had struggled with a profound fear of death. I don't know why this was or how it began. I had no traumatic experiences with death in my early childhood that I am aware of. The fear just quietly took hold of my imagination until I had no memory of living without the constant awareness that I am going to die. I will leave my body, and it will become cold and still. I will lose contact with the people and the things that I love. Death, that threatening predator, will seize me and throw me into darkness alone.

Not that I lived morbidly or became depressed. This fear did not paralyze my days, my childhood play, my growth into womanhood, my energy in preparing for a nursing career, my joy in marrying and bearing children. I loved the Lord; my days belonged to him. But my nights belonged to fear.

As soon as I lay down and the world was dark, as soon as sleep claimed my children and my husband—always long before me—then the dread voice would reverberate through my mind: "You're going to die." I was afraid to yield to sleep, that foreshadowing of death. Sometimes the mantra brought with it malicious suggestions. "What's the point? You're going to have to die. Why go on waiting for the inevitable? End it yourself; at least the fear will be over."

A devout Catholic, I recognized this as oppression from the Evil One. Moreover, as a charismatic Christian I knew that the Holy Spirit could save me from this torment. I had seen many people healed, delivered and set free. I prayed that he would do it for me too.

For years I prayed. I asked people to pray over me, to rebuke the enemy, to walk the corridors of memory with me and to minister inner healing to that fearful little girl. But nothing ever changed.

After several years of desperate doubt, when my heart questioned God's actual involvement in my small life, I finally reached a place of surrender. I knew I had asked the Lord many times for healing and would continue to ask, but I also accepted the fact that for some reason, the Lord was allowing me to carry this cross, a form of suffering beyond my control.

So in the dark nights, instead of cowering and begging God for release, I just expressed my trust in the Lord and offered him my pain. "Use this, Lord, to help your people and to help me grow in love for you. Walk with me in this terror; I know you are here."

One night, just after I prayed this prayer, my room was filled with a golden light. Suddenly I saw myself lying not on my own bed but on what I knew was my deathbed. I lay peacefully, surrounded by that gentle light. The room was full of people, and I knew them— angels, special saints I had prayed to all my life, my heavenly mother and also the souls of dear friends who had already passed on.

My soul lifted from my body and was welcomed by all these happy beings crowding around me. We walked together into what seemed like just the next room, but I knew that this was the next world, where I would soon meet Jesus. Then the vision faded—but not the light—and I was back in my bed.

The Holy Spirit then spoke clearly to my soul three declarations, with a powerful pause between each one: *It will not be violent. It will not be dark. You will not be alone.*

Since that moment I have experienced no fear of death. The Lord marvelously, unexpectedly and without the intervention of another soul addressed the roots of my fear and set me free.

For me this experience underlines the verse: "Where the Spirit of the Lord is, there is freedom" (2 Corinthians 3:17). My only part is to yield my entire body, heart, soul, intellect, memory and imagination to his loving will, day and night.

A Special Baby
—Nancy from Michigan

Our son Joseph was born with serious heart defects and placed on life support in the neonatal intensive care unit. We visited him whenever we could. The evening of his fourth day was especially difficult; Joseph just didn't look good. Not only was he hooked up to many tubes, but he also seemed distressed, especially when the nurse suctioned him.

I knew this was a very uncomfortable procedure, because as a nurse myself I had done it to adult patients. Joseph would have such a pitiful, pained look, and he would cry and cry, even though he couldn't make a sound with the respirator tube down his throat. It just broke my heart, and I felt helpless.

I wanted to comfort my son. I tried touching his feet, but immediately his oxygen saturation level dropped. The nurse said we should avoid any stimulation at all for a while, even touching him. My husband and I decided to just go home. It had been another long, emotionally draining day, and I couldn't take any more.

When I got home and into bed, I started to pray and cry and desperately ask God to help my son and to comfort and care for him. I started to drop off to sleep, when suddenly I saw a picture in my mind. It was of a woman and two young girls, around the age of thirteen, with a small baby.

The woman was standing between the girls, who were taking turns holding the baby. Their faces were full of joy, delighting in caring for this little baby. They oohed and aahed and giggled over him. And he in turn responded to them, his face full of peace and contentment.

The picture seemed real and was full of detail. I immediately knew it was Mary and two angels sent to take care of Joseph and comfort him. God allowed me to see his answer to my prayer; he had sent these to care for and comfort my son.

A sense of peace washed over me. Even though Joseph's body was still full of tubes, in some divine way his spirit was being cared for, being comforted by his holy mother and the angels.

Some years later, around the holidays, I opened a Christmas card and started crying. The picture on the card was exactly like the image I had seen. Mary and two angels surrounded the Christ Child. Their faces were the same as what I remembered.

I have this picture often in my heart. It helps me remember and appreciate God's great love and mercy for giving us Joseph and saving him—and for giving us all Jesus and saving us. How great is God's love for us, and how he delights over each of us!

God's Consoling Presence
—Michèle from Michigan

One of the ways the Holy Spirit works in my life is to make me more aware of heaven breaking into earth. With this the Spirit brings a profound, tangible peace and comfort.

Two notable examples of this occurred when I was dealing with my husband's cancer. Tim was diagnosed in 2000 with an incurable brain tumor, and he was given a prognosis of three to five years, even with the most aggressive treatment.

Tim's initial symptoms were tingling in his left hand and foot, which lasted for quite a while. He was hospitalized as a precaution until the doctors could fit him into the MRI schedule to make a diagnosis. They thought he probably had had a mild stroke.

Tim's hospitalization was difficult for me. On one level I was deeply concerned for Tim and wanted to stay with him all the time. But I knew I had to keep things on as normal a schedule as possible for our two young adopted daughters. Any change for them was stressful, and they had recently gone through a lot of change! My fear was that having already lost their birth parents, their adoptive father was now ill.

Driving home from the hospital one day, I sensed the Holy Spirit stirring. The realization came to me that Tim's problem could be a brain tumor. I knew that this thought was from the Holy Spirit, because with it came a deep calm and peace. The worry from Tim's sudden hospitalization left me.

On the way to the hospital the next morning, I dropped my daughters off with friends. My three-year-old, only recently adopted, normally wouldn't leave me, not even to stay with Tim. Yet she happily chose to stay with these friends and play. This caught my attention, and I pondered it on the way to the hospital.

"Hmmm. Something is going on. Lord, what are you doing?" I wondered. I knew that the Holy Spirit was orchestrating things and going ahead of me, and I was not afraid.

When I arrived at the hospital, I took one look at Tim's face and knew there was something seriously wrong. "I have good news and bad news," he said.

Wanting to end things on a good note, I asked for the bad first. "I have a brain tumor," he said. I took him in my arms and told him it was OK. He started crying out of relief from the fear of telling me and of how I would react.

Though Tim admitted that he really didn't have any good news, we both knew with the deepest peace that we were in a win-win situation—whether Tim lived or went to be with the Lord. We prayed confidently, "Thy will be done." There wasn't any fear, just the heavenly peace and calm the Holy Spirit gives.

This peace was even more pronounced the day the tumor was biopsied. It was deep in Tim's brain, so there was a risk of permanent brain damage. I kissed him good-bye, not knowing whether I would see him alive or well again. Yet as they wheeled him into the operating room, I was filled with peace and stillness!

I felt as if I could reach out and touch the Lord; the sense of his presence was that strong. The physical world of the hospital was still around me, but the reality of God's presence was more tangible. I knew he was my Lord and in full control. The power of the Holy Spirit permeated my world. The best way I can think of describing it is that heaven was breaking into earth.

Since then the Lord has worked powerfully to bless my husband's health. And this experience of the Holy Spirit gently breaking into my life has helped me to understand more deeply how the Holy Spirit gently breaks into earth and brings Jesus to us during the consecration at Mass.

With Him or Without Him?

—*Jack from Michigan*

Shortly after my wife and I were married, we received the good news that she was pregnant. We were, of course, very excited, looking forward to this new phase of our life together. However, about halfway through the pregnancy, Lisa's water broke, and we rushed to the hospital. The hospital staff confirmed our fears as soon as we arrived: Lisa was miscarrying.

The staff moved Lisa into a delivery room as quickly as possible, while we hoped and prayed that the doctors were wrong. To our astonishment our baby was born, obviously dead, as we waited for the nurse to return. I remember my shock at seeing my first child, a boy perfectly formed in most ways already. I had a fleeting glimpse of his face and then he was gone, whisked away by a perhaps overly attentive nurse who wanted to spare us some trauma.

In my dejection and grief I went downstairs to the chapel to pray and seek God. I was heartbroken. That glimpse of my son's face had captured my heart, and he was gone before I had a chance even to hold him, let alone ever know him. Wasn't God supposed to protect us from this kind of thing?

As I sat there in the chapel, asking the Lord to help me understand what was going on, I sensed him in my heart, speaking more clearly than I ever had heard before. I sensed his saying to me, "This is a difficult time. You are going to have to go through it one way or another. Do you want to go through it with me or without me?"

I didn't hesitate for a moment. "Lord," I prayed, "I don't want this to drive a wedge between us. I choose to go through it with you."

I decided this would be a good time to ask the Lord for a passage from Scripture, something I didn't do very often. So I opened my Bible to Isaiah 44:3–5:

> I will pour my Spirit upon your descendants,
>   and my blessing on your offspring.
> They shall spring up like grass amid waters,
>   like willows by flowing streams.
> This one will say, "I am the LORD's,"
>   another will call himself by the name of Jacob,
>   and another will write on his hand, "The LORD's,"
>   and surname himself by the name of Israel.

I was amazed, to say the least; it was the exact word I needed for the situation I was in.

In the next few years my wife and I would need that promise. We seemed unable to get pregnant again, and we feared there was something wrong. But our faith and the prayers of many friends were rewarded with the birth of a son, and soon after that another.

The Lord's word to me that day became a spiritual bedrock for my life. We had four more miscarriages to endure before ending up with five precious children in all, and I went through a string of job losses at one point. Whenever I was confronted with a difficult situation, I remembered the Lord's question to me from that night and chose again to go through the hard time with him, staying close to him in prayer.

And his promise was golden: All five of our children either are or are growing up to be solid and committed in their faith as Catholics, knowing that Christ himself is the heart of their faith in the power of the Holy Spirit.

Something Dark Has Been Lifted

—Betty from Michigan

My twelve-year-old son, Justin, and I attend a church that is very open to the gifts of the Holy Spirit. One Sunday morning we were sitting separately at church during a half hour or so of worship. I sensed the presence of the Holy Spirit very strongly that morning through the music.

Our pastor suggested that we take time to pray with our family members, right then and there. As soon as he finished speaking, it was very clear what

I needed to do; I had no fear or trepidation. The Holy Spirit wanted me to go find Justin.

It had been a difficult time for us recently as we dealt with Justin's Attention Deficit Hyperactivity Disorder and its medications. The challenges that come with adolescence hadn't made it any easier. Evenings and weekends were especially difficult as the medications wore off, and my son would become argumentative and impulsive. Family tensions would escalate, leaving everyone miserable.

When I found Justin, I drew him toward the back of the church. Tears were streaming down my face. "I'm sorry that I've been yelling at you lately, Justin," I said.

Right away he responded, "I'm sorry, too, Mom." His voice was sincere. We both said, "I love you."

We didn't have to say a lot more to each other; we both understood what we meant. We hugged each other, and I had the strong impression that something had been resolved. It all happened very quickly, but something significant had occurred between us, something that was a gift from the Holy Spirit.

Since that morning my relationship with Justin has definitely improved. There's less tension and arguing in the evenings. There's a different dynamic now when we're in the same room together; it's almost as if something dark has been lifted.

Unless God does a miracle, the ADHD isn't going to disappear anytime soon, but this experience helped me see that the Holy Spirit would help us to cope with it. One day Justin was home sick, so he didn't take his medication. In spite of that the day was harmonious. A couple of times Justin came up to me and gave me a hug, saying, "I really want you to know that I appreciate everything you do for me."

It seems as though the Holy Spirit is working in Justin's heart. I know that his behavior isn't completely voluntary, and he can't simply decide to start acting differently. Still there seems to be at least some voluntary component that is changing for the better. It all started that Sunday at church, when Justin wanted me to know what was truly in his heart underneath all the external behaviors.

Spiritual Healing

—Pat from New Jersey

I had been attending a Life in the Spirit Seminar for several weeks. Through a personal experience with the Holy Spirit, I had begun to experience a joy and peace I had never known. My husband Ed was happy to see this newfound joy and calm in me. I invited him to join me for the seminar's closing Mass.

Approximately forty people attended the Mass. We sang and prayed in tongues, our hands open and raised in worship. At this time, in the early 1970s, this was a new way of worshiping during Mass. Everyone in attendance truly believed in the presence of the Lord, with the sole exception of my husband.

As we left to go home, Ed became incensed over what he had just seen and experienced. He shouted,

"You are all crazy." The rage within him festered throughout the rest of the day. On his way to bed that night, he threatened that if I should ever mention the name of Jesus in our home again, he would leave. Having two small children at this time, I was frightened.

I knew in my heart that Jesus was Lord over my life and that he was calling me to trust in him. I sought the Blessed Mother's intercession that night and experienced peace. Neither Ed nor I slept; I prayed, while he tossed and turned. At 4:00 AM he left for work in the middle of a snowstorm, an hour and a half earlier than his usual departure time. I continued to pray all day, not knowing what he would be like when he returned.

When Ed arrived home that evening, he was still very angry, and I knew that we were in the midst of a spiritual battle. Satan was not going to give up easily.

At one point I turned to Ed and asked him if his behavior made any sense. He stopped and looked at me with fear in his eyes and said that he did not understand what was happening to him. I pleaded with him to say the Our Father with me. He agreed. The anger within him dissipated, and he wept.

This was the beginning of a spiritual healing for Ed. The road was long and bumpy, as he had endless doubts. However, he came to weekly Mass and prayer meetings. In time he accepted Jesus as his Savior and was baptized in the Holy Spirit.

Ed reiterated many times that if it were not for my faith and persistence, he would have given up his spiritual journey. Today we go on mission trips, and we share our testimony on the saving power of the Holy Spirit.

Why Is There a Dove in My Room?
—Jerri from Arkansas

When our twelve-year-old son David was diagnosed with a malignant brain tumor, my orderly, secure life was suddenly uprooted. Everything that I thought I knew and believed about God's care for his children came into question. My heart was so paralyzed with fear that I was unable to pray.

I was baptized Catholic as an infant and raised by a devout mother who loved the Lord. I thought that I had been practicing my faith fully for thirty-seven years. Our family attended Mass every Sunday and said grace before meals. Every morning I led my boys in prayer on the way to school, just as my mother had done for me.

Yet on that frightening February day, I realized that my spiritual foundation was not deep enough to withstand this trial. I knew I needed more help, strength, courage and hope than I could muster on my own.

I was enrolled in my first Bible study class at the time, so I instantly reached for God's Word and searched for something more to sustain me. We had begun studying the Gospel of John in class just the day before. In John 1:23 John the Baptist proclaims, "I am 'the voice of one crying out in the desert, / "Make straight the way of the Lord!"'" (*New American Bible*).

That word spoke to my heart, because I was definitely feeling "deserted" by God, and now I was "crying out" for the Lord's help. I desperately wanted the Lord to show me the way to him, for I knew that I needed his strength to get through this ordeal with David. God's Word let me know that he was with me. It confirmed to me that the Holy Spirit was guiding my steps, for he brought that Scripture to my mind just when I needed it. "Make straight the way of the Lord!" became my prayer.

Enduring David's ten-hour brain surgery was terrifying. I was so fearful that he would not survive it or not emerge from the ordeal the same boy I knew and loved so dearly. The only prayer that seemed to come effortlessly was, "The LORD is my shepherd; I shall not want" (Psalm 23:1). This prayerful mantra slowly began to calm my anxious spirit.

As the day wore on, many family members and friends from church gathered around us in the hospital waiting room. Their loving support and prayers helped us get through that long day.

When the doctor finally came into the waiting room late that evening, he estimated that he had removed 80 percent of the tumor. He was amazed that David had even been able to function with so much of the tumor invading his brain. It was clear to me that

David's battle was not over, but he was strong and fighting, and for that I was extremely grateful.

Early the next morning I sought out the hospital chapel in order to spend some quiet time there. The sight that greeted me was a beautiful, larger-than-life, stained-glass window of Jesus the Good Shepherd. The light streaming in from behind the window made the colors glow gloriously. As I gazed at it longer, I imagined that the small lamb that the Shepherd was caressing so tenderly in his arms was my David.

That image alone would have been enough to strengthen me that day, but the Holy Spirit had more in store for me. My attention was directed immediately toward the large Bible on a lectionary stand at the front of the chapel. It was opened to Psalm 27, and I began to read: "The LORD is my light and my salvation; / whom shall I fear? / The LORD is the stronghold of my life; / of whom shall I be afraid?"

I held on to the image of the window and that Scripture as the days and weeks went by. I read the Psalms often. My heart focused on the verse, "Wait for the LORD; / be strong, and let your heart take courage; / yes, wait for the LORD!" (Psalm 27:14). The Holy Spirit had filled my heart with a hope that helped sustain me through the weeks of physical recovery and radiation treatments for David.

About two weeks after his surgery, David was released from the hospital. Each weekday morning he and I would attend Mass at our parish and then drive across town for his radiation treatment. In the beginning I struggled to remain positive and courageous for David's sake. David, however, appeared to be unconcerned; in fact, he seemed to be thriving.

Oftentimes on the way there David would break into song. His favorite was "This is the day which the Lord has made. Let us be glad and rejoice in it" from Psalm 118. At the hospital he would cheerily greet the staff by name, as if they were all good friends. Everyone was amazed at his joy during this time. I know that it was an answer to all the prayers that were being offered on his behalf and a true gift of grace from the Holy Spirit. This was a faith-building time for me.

Following the six weeks of radiation, we met with an oncologist, and he prescribed a six-month chemotherapy regimen for David. After four months the chemotherapy was shown to be ineffective at reducing the remaining tumor. So the doctors recommended their last medical option, a bone marrow transplant.

In the midst of all these frightening circumstances, the Holy Spirit continued to minister to my spirit in many ways. He led me to just the right Scripture verse when a difficult decision had to be made; he prompted my friends to write or call with encouragement when I was despairing; he filled my soul with a comforting hymn when my mind was consumed with worry. There was never any doubt that the Holy

Spirit was with me, leading me to the abundant love that Jesus was offering.

At the outset I prayed that the Lord would give me strength, but the Holy Spirit knew that was not enough. He wanted to take me into a much deeper relationship with my Lord. He was gently persistent in his leading, and I expectantly complied because I could feel the love pulling me deeper, grounding me in hope. It was where I knew I belonged, walking daily beside my Lord Jesus.

Just a week out of isolation from his transplant, David relapsed. As I entered his hospital room and moved closer to his bed, David spoke.

"Mom? Is that you? Where were you?"

"I thought you were sleeping, so I stepped down the hall to the atrium."

As I was talking to David, he never turned his head to look at me or even opened his eyes. I kept talking, hoping that he would begin to respond more fully. Then he asked the question that I had been dreading, as I had tried hard during the past nine months to shield him from the harsh reality of his illness.

"Mom, why am I having such a hard time getting well?"

From somewhere within me the answer came, and yet the words sounded foreign to my own ears—almost as if someone else had spoken them. "Well, David, maybe it's because you just don't need this body of yours anymore."

Then something miraculous happened. David

opened his eyes. And looking intently at the ceiling above his bed, he asked, "Why is there a dove in my room?"

I looked up but saw only ceiling tiles. I began to realize what had just taken place. In one sacred moment when reality had questioned faith, the answer had not come from me. It had been the Holy Spirit who had answered. He simply had used my voice.

Within a week David's condition had stabilized, and we were able to take him home. Two and a half months later, on a quiet morning in February, a year after this ordeal had begun, I was sitting at my kitchen table spending time in God's Word. This had now become my daily habit, seeking the Holy Spirit's guidance before starting my day. I turned my Bible to the Scripture passage for that day; Hebrews 12 gave me an awesome vision.

There were angels in heaven wearing festive robes, waiting to greet David, and Jesus was there to welcome him home. Suddenly I realized that death was not to be feared. I knew that it was time for me to let David go. Even up to the very end, the gentle, loving Holy Spirit was still helping me, giving me the grace to accept God's plan for David.

Now, when I look back on that year's difficult journey, it seems perfectly natural that the Holy Spirit would have been by my side to walk through it with me. Since my baptism the Holy Spirit had been with me, and at my confirmation he had fully instilled his gifts within me.

It had been my mistake to overlook the Spirit all those years and not seek the full power and potential of his gifts in my life. I allowed those gifts to lie dormant within me until painful circumstances finally forced me to call out to the Lord for help. My faithful Lord sent his Helper to me, just as he had promised before he left the earth.

CHAPTER FIVE

The Power to Heal

The power of the Lord was with him to heal.

Luke 5:17

We Could Hear the Crackling in His Lungs

—Donna from Canada

In the spring of 1995, our twelve-year-old son suddenly began to experience severe allergy problems, the most serious of which was asthma. This prevented him from running, playing sports and walking any distance, even with the help of medication. He was drained of any semblance of energy. When we stood next to him, we readily could hear the wheezing and crackling in his lungs.

As my husband and I prayed for our son, we could not help but feel that this asthma was not God's will for him. So we asked him if he wanted to go to a healing service to ask Jesus to heal him. He responded enthusiastically to this suggestion. We felt the Lord calling us to attend the next healing service at our parish.

During the prayer service the priest offered to anoint the sick with oil. My husband and I made our way to the altar with our son. Father welcomed us with a warm smile and hug, and as the choir sang "Peace Is Flowing Like a River," tears started streaming down our son's cheeks.

Father anointed him with the holy oil, and he instantly fell down under the power of the Holy Spirit. After some time he began to lean on one elbow in an attempt to get up. Father emerged and anointed him again, and once more our son rested in the Spirit.

After a long while he got up, profoundly filled with peace and *totally healed of asthma and other allergies!* Our wonderful, loving God had restored our boy to total health. Sitting next to him in the pew while he regained strength, we could no longer hear any crackling noise in his chest.

Our son discontinued his medication that very night. Six weeks later, on our way to an appointment with our family doctor, I asked him what he was going to say. He stated that he would tell the doctor that the Lord Jesus had healed him of the asthma and allergies at a healing service.

That is precisely what he did! The doctor proceeded to listen closely to his lungs and chest, and she was amazed. Truly his asthma was healed. She was impressed by the fact that, despite the extreme humidity of the summer, which would surely worsen an asthma condition, his lungs were exceptionally clear. We rejoiced and gave thanks and praise to our ever-loving and compassionate God.

God Came to Visit Us

—Tom from Florida

It began on a Monday evening in a small prayer group in Tampa, Florida, in 1971. My wife Pam and I had been married for four years, and we had two beautiful children. I was working in a management position with a large retail shoe company. We had been married in the Catholic church, and I was raised Catholic, but our practice of the faith during our first years of marriage had been infrequent and superficial at best.

So why were we now sitting here among thirty strangers who were singing and praying in a way that made me uncomfortable but seemed to be a great joy to them? I was already having reservations about telling that little nun who had met us at the door that I would agree to come to this meeting three times. Going to a prayer meeting was not on my list of "things to do this week."

I was there only because Pam had talked me into accompanying her. Pam was there because she was searching for something. For the previous two years she had been living with the very disabling disease called lupus. The doctors had given us a dim prognosis for her future. Now, through a series of events, we found ourselves in the midst of this seemingly strange gathering of priests, nuns and laypeople. In retrospect it was the hand of God that guided us there.

We found ourselves returning each Monday evening. Although not yet comfortable, my uneasiness was beginning to dissipate. It had something to do with the genuine affection shared among this little band of people.

For several weeks Pam and I would go to a corner of the room, and Earl, a young Jesuit seminarian, would give us some instruction from the Life in the Spirit Seminar. During each session he would share two or three Scripture passages. My experience with the Bible up to that point was practically nonexistent. When Pam and I were married, someone gave us one of those big white Catholic Bibles, which immediately became a centerpiece on our coffee table. We used it to hold photos and other papers, and perhaps once in a while I browsed the beautiful color pictures depicting Bible scenes.

But now, as Earl pointed out a Scripture passage, the words seemed to slice into my inner being despite the wall that I was still working to keep up. The words seemed to have a life of their own, and deep down within me began a slow realization that these words were truth. These words began to answer questions about life, perhaps ones that I never had allowed to surface but had held inside.

At home I began to pick up the big Bible on the coffee table and read entire sections. Suddenly it was like today's news but far better than anything in the daily paper. Pam also was reading and praying fervently. We found ourselves talking to Jesus as though he were standing beside us, and we began to experience a presence within, the Holy Spirit.

The little prayer group did a lot of praying for healing of friends and loved ones and offered special prayers for healing among those present. One Monday night they gathered around Pam, laid their hands upon her and began to pray just as Jesus had instructed his followers to pray.

That night we fell asleep knowing that Pam had a doctor's appointment the next morning at the university clinic. At about three o'clock in the morning, I was suddenly wide awake and sitting up in bed. Pam also awakened. I found myself exclaiming, "He's here!"

The room was filled with an awesome presence. Pam felt a heat going through her body and began to cry. We both knew that God had come to visit us and that something was happening. The presence lasted several minutes, but there was no more sleep that night. At 5:30 AM we were up and off to the clinic.

When Pam met with her doctor, she explained to him the whole story—our involvement in a prayer meeting, the Scripture, the prayer the night before and the experience during the night. She said, "I think I have been healed."

The doctor conducted all of the tests that were a part of each visit, and we went home to wait for the results. In a couple of hours the doctor called us and said, "It's gone; the tests are negative." He wrote on her chart: "Lupus healed." Since that day the lupus has never reappeared.

In the early days of her sickness Pam had prayed that she might live to see her children graduate from high school. Now she greatly enjoys the blessings of six grandchildren.

Earth-Shattering News
—Anonymous

I was raised in a devout Catholic family, yet we never talked openly about our faith in the home. My parents were devoted to the sacraments, but they considered faith a private matter. Throughout my childhood and young adult life, the fear of God was always stressed, but I never heard much about the personal, loving side of God.

I attended Catholic schools and went to Georgetown, a Catholic university. I met and married a good Catholic man, and we began to raise our children Catholic, just as my parents had. I often prayed for the protection of my children, but mostly God seemed distant and impersonal.

Six years ago, when my son Steven was almost four years old, he came down with a strep throat infection that traveled into his bloodstream and began to eat away at a bone in his foot. He was hospitalized for five days and put on intravenous antibiotics. It was a stressful time for our family, but we were optimistic about his recovery, placing our hope in the doctors' care. I didn't think much about turning to God for help.

Little Steven spent the next six weeks on an antibiotic catheter. One week after his treatment ended, he began to complain of pains in his arms, ribs and foot. He had a fever and couldn't move.

After a series of blood tests and exams, the doctors diagnosed Steven with leukemia. We were told he would have to undergo three years and two months of chemotherapy. We had no time to process this earth-shattering news.

That first night back in the hospital, I began to ask God why he was allowing an innocent child to suffer. I felt abandoned by God and was full of despair and sorrow. I began to question everything. Was God real? Did he even care about us? My husband and I prayed together and asked God to give Steven healing and strength and not to let him suffer.

Two days later a friend called, and I told her that I felt God had abandoned me. She said in a very matter-of-fact tone, "Don't expect to understand this ordeal; you're not meant to. Just give yourself to God and say to him, 'Take me and show me.'"

That night I sat on the couch in Steven's hospital room, closed my eyes and began to talk to God in a way I never had before. "I don't understand why I feel so lost," I said, "and I don't know what to do for my son. Please take me and show me." I reached my arms out to God and simply surrendered to him, saying, "I'm yours."

Suddenly warmth came over my fingers, my arms, my whole body. It was a tangible warmth on the outside that permeated deep into my being. With it came an indescribable peace, and all my anxiety left.

I sat there not wanting to move. This warmth and peace was followed by a sense of great love, and I knew without a doubt that it was my Lord touching me and loving me and telling me, "I am here." I began to cry.

My immediate response to this great love was a desire to love God in return. I was filled with a tremendous joy; it was beyond any happiness I had ever known.

I then had an acute awareness of Steven's presence and his suffering. I sensed I was to go over to his bed and place my hands gently on his small body. As I did this, warmth from within me went out to Steven. I knew it was the power of the Lord's healing, renewing Steven's health and his life.

That encounter with the Lord and his Holy Spirit completely changed my faith life. God was there all along, yet he was waiting for me to surrender myself to him so I could know him in a personal, intimate way. I now have an insatiable hunger for God, to know him and to know how I can serve him. I read and study the Bible daily, and I see a whole new dimension to the sacraments and the life of the church. I have a new perspective on raising my children, one that includes helping them know Jesus personally and the importance of prayer.

As for Steven, we prayed together before each treatment, and he sailed heroically through his chemotherapy and into remission. His recent six-year follow-up visit to the doctor found him to be a healthy, strong, normal ten-year-old boy with lots of energy and a deep love for God.

It Happened—Quietly, Quickly, Unexpectedly
—Anne from Canada

In the fall of 2002, I started to have a lot of pain in my lower back. My physician recommended anti-inflammatory medication and physiotherapy, which did not help. Within weeks I was having difficulty walking, and I eventually lost the reflexes in my right leg. The pain became so bad that the doctor put me on medications that dulled my senses so that I was unable to work. But even these did not do much to control the pain.

I could walk only with the assistance of a cane, and even with that not very far. I couldn't drive and couldn't sit down for very long. I didn't sleep well and was in constant pain.

An MRI showed a condition called spondyliothesis, caused by acute arthritis that had worn out the facet joints in my vertebrae. The back specialist recommended some spinal epidural injections, which did nothing. The next step was surgery. In the meantime the pain was making me miserable and short-tempered with my family.

One night at a prayer meeting, the group saw the state I was in and gathered to pray for my healing. Nothing appeared to happen; I was still in pain. But after a few days, I noticed that I was no longer short-tempered with my family. I recalled that when I was being prayed with, what was in my heart was that I didn't want the short-temperedness from my pain to cause my family pain. I ended up being in pain for over seven months, but never again was I short-tempered with my family. This was a wonderful grace!

During Lent of 2003 I attended our parish mission. I went to morning Mass each day of the mission, and one day after Communion I had an interior vision. The Lord Jesus came to me and picked me up in his arms. He carried me with outstretched arms to the Father and said, "Father, this is your beloved daughter, and even though she is in a lot of pain, she still serves us, and because of this I will heal her."

This type of thing had never happened to me before, and I was convinced that I would be healed. After Mass I went up to the celebrant, a bishop, and told him about the vision and that I believed I would be healed.

I was in such bad shape at that time that I had rails installed on my bed to help me turn over and get up. I spent hours just hanging over an exercise ball, in tears, trying to relieve the pain, and I was taking the dose of painkiller used to treat cancer patients.

Then it happened, quietly, quickly and unexpectedly. I went to my prayer meeting early and was praying before the Blessed Sacrament. My hands felt as if they were being anointed, and the Lord prompted me to go and pray for one of the other members of the prayer group. This person had heart problems and was scheduled for surgery in the next couple of days.

I laid my hands on this man and prayed in tongues. I could feel the power of the Spirit moving through my hands to him, and he said to me, "Now I know I will be OK."

Then he started to pray for me, and I could feel the power of the Spirit coming through his hands. It was like a little whirlwind, with the Holy Spirit moving between the two of us, going out from me to him and also from him to me. This continued for a couple of minutes.

When I went home that night, I was tired and forgot to take my painkillers. When I woke in the morning, the pain was completely gone.

What fruit this healing bore! In my parish I am a cantor, so I cross in front of the altar, in the sight of everyone, to chant the psalm from the ambo. Everyone in our large parish had seen me struggling for over seven months to get to the ambo to sing. From one Sunday to the next they saw me without my cane and walking normally, and everyone wanted to know what had happened. I had numerous opportunities to evangelize through this healing, and it was powerful. For many people it brought the realization that God is alive and working and healing today.

A Fireman Encounters the Healing Lord

—*Ken from New Jersey*

As a fireman in 1960, I was responding to an alarm when I fractured two vertebrae in my spine. I spent ten days in the hospital, and not wishing to have an operation, I exercised to strengthen the muscles in my back. Everything was fine for three years.

One day I went to pick up my wife, who was a nurse at the hospital, and I ran into my orthopedic doctor. He asked me to come and see him. He said that I needed an operation or I would end up crippled. I had started to limp and not even realized it.

Needless to say, I agreed to the surgery, which was performed in November 1963. The doctors took a piece of my hip to fuse together vertebrae L4 and L5, but something went very wrong. They left a sponge in me, and I hemorrhaged so severely post-op that I had to go back into surgery.

My first surgery began at 11:00 AM, and the second surgery ended at 1:00 AM. In this second surgery the doctors removed all the fused pieces to locate the sponge, which had allowed large amounts of air to get into my spinal column. It was a very serious condition. My head swelled to the size of a volleyball, and I was in a comatose state, with tubes in every orifice of my body. All my organs began to shut down. I was dying.

On November 22, 1963, I awoke, sat up in bed and rang for a nurse to tell her I was hungry. When she saw me she looked as if she was going to faint. I went home ten days later, did rehab for six months and then went back to a job that I loved. Everything was fine for sixteen years.

On November 2, 1979, the Feast of All Souls, I was working a multihouse fire at two o'clock in the morning when I fell through a few floors and shattered my spine again. I spent ten days in the hospital, and then I was sent to Columbia Presbyterian Hospital in New York City for another operation, which I did not want. A lady I met there gave me tapes on healing by Father Ralph Diario.

The surgeon was pushing me to have surgery. I said I would think about it, and he warned me not to take too long in deciding, or I would lose the use of my right leg, wear a brace on it and end up in a wheelchair. At that time I was wearing a steel brace from midback to midthigh. I went home unable to do anything and in constant pain. I was going into a deep depression.

My wife and I decided to go see Father Diario in Massachusetts. When we arrived the church was so crowded that people were standing in the aisles. My wife found two seats in the balcony. I could hear

Father but could not see him.

Father Diario, in a word of knowledge, began describing my spinal injury and leg problem. He said, "He is a tall man, and he is sitting upstairs in the balcony."

At that time I felt a twinge in my back. I walked to the rail and saw Father standing directly under me. He raised a large cross and asked me, "Do you want to be healed?" I said, "Yes, I want to be healed," and he said, "In the name of Jesus, be healed."

I took off my brace, drove back to New Jersey and put the brace in the attic. I played eighteen holes of golf the next day. I remain totally healed and free from pain.

The day of my healing was May 1, 1980, the first day of the month dedicated to Our Lady.

Holding Hands and Praising God

—"Butch" Robert from Michigan

One Friday night, while my wife and I were on a weekend retreat at Marygrove Retreat House, I went to confession. As the priest stood up to pray over me, he placed his hand over my head, and my face felt hot and glowing. The heat was intense and warm. That night I slept peacefully with "nothing on my mind." I felt that the Holy Spirit was blessing me.

The next morning, during one of the talks, I felt as if the speaker was talking directly to me about my life. I realized that God has a real purpose for me, that God wants me to pay more attention to his Word and that the Holy Spirit wants me to witness to others. I felt lifted up, brand new and grace-filled.

On Sunday morning the leader asked if anyone wanted to share anything. I said that I was never able to sleep with the left side of my face on the pillow because of the diabetic neuropathy I have on that side. The pain is normally too intolerable. My wife shared that when she awakened that morning, she saw me sleeping peacefully with that side of my face on the pillow. I then awoke, and we were so filled with joy that we just stayed there in bed, holding hands and praising God.

I went on to explain that I used to have so much pain on the left side of my face that I couldn't even touch it with my hand without it hurting. As I said this, I slapped my left cheek and laughed with joy!

Another Year to Serve the Lord
—*Gerald from Michigan*

I was born into a Catholic family, though not an overly devout one. I attended Mass regularly and received the sacraments. My own children attended Catholic schools, and we all attended Mass regularly.

Sometime during 1969 I developed a severe case of sciatica. I went to two orthopedic surgeons, and both said that deteriorating spinal discs were causing vertebrae to press on my sciatic nerve. This would in time necessitate surgery. My condition became progressively worse, until I could not walk any distance or stand more than a minute or two without serious pain.

I returned to work after a one-month medical leave, but the physical problem continued for about seven years. I spent my evenings sitting on the couch watching television or reading.

One night I looked up at our bookshelf, and my eyes lit on a Bible that I had bought at a book sale a few years before. I had never really read the Bible before. I removed it from the shelf and began reading the Gospel of Saint Matthew.

When I came to the ministry of Jesus and began to read his words, I stopped and thought, *I am going to read this as Jesus speaking to me personally.* The Scriptures began to come alive to me. I found myself unable to put down the Bible. After this I began sitting up until one o'clock in the morning reading, absorbing the words and stories of Jesus!

One day between Christmas and New Year's of 1976, I was sitting in the living room listening to music on the radio. The room was dark except for the lights on our Christmas tree. As I gazed at a plaster statuette of the Last Supper under the tree, I focused on the figure of Jesus and thought about that last night before his death. Thoughts of my own mortality began racing through my mind, and a thought from outside of me came: "Are you ready to leave, to die?" I tried to shake off the thought, but it kept turning around in my mind.

It was then that Jesus spoke to my heart. He told me that he really loved me and that he became a man and went to the cross, dying in my place, taking the punishment for my sins, so that I could be with him forever. I had heard all my life that Jesus died for the sins of the world, but it never occurred to me that he died for my sins because he loves me!

In retrospect I know that the Holy Spirit was revealing to me the basic truth of salvation and giving me a responsive heart that night. Right then and there I thanked Jesus from the bottom of my heart for loving me and dying for me. I told him I loved him and wanted everyone to know that I loved him. I invited Jesus into my heart and asked him to live his life in me. That night I fell asleep in perfect peace, with no fear of dying!

A few days later, on New Year's Day, my family and I attended Mass. The priest began by saying, "My brothers and sisters, let us give thanks to the Lord that he has given us another year in which to serve him!" It was as though the Lord was speaking directly to me! I said a prayer in my heart: "Lord, if it is only one year, then I want it to be all for you!"

Later in January I began attending a charismatic prayer meeting at a local Catholic church. Because of the disabling sciatic problem, I was anointed with blessed oil and prayed over for healing. Within a period of eight months, after having suffered eight years of pain, the Lord totally healed me of the problem!

Toxic Mold Meets the Holy Spirit

—Carol from Michigan

In the early 1990s I had a mysterious illness that took me lower each year, to a point where I was in excruciating pain and had difficulty taking care of the ordinary tasks of life. I was in graduate studies at Sacred Heart Major Seminary in Detroit and had to drop three major classes just before the end of the semester in 1999. I was too weak and sick to continue.

I gave my life to the Lord to do with as he willed, and suddenly the long-sought answers began to come. The source of my illness was discovered to be the presence of toxic mold in our home, which was slowly poisoning me. We remedied the situation, and I began to regain strength, but not without some permanent lung damage from the long-term exposure.

I returned to graduate school with full-time status in the fall of 2003, and with great joy I registered for a class that I had wanted to take. After the first day I knew that I was going to have trouble with the classroom. The newly installed carpet was causing serious inflammation in my lungs. It was hard work to draw air in, and when I did, the air felt like fire in my lungs.

At the end of the second week, I went to speak with the professor about dropping the class. He asked me if I would like to pray for healing. With some hesitation I agreed. He began to pray in English and then prayed in a most beautiful language, one I had never heard.

Something marvelous happened! All the cares and baggage I had accumulated during my life seemed to be lifted away, and I felt great peace and joy. I told my professor what had happened and thanked him. He said to let him know if anything further happened.

Later that day I was walking down the long corridor out of the seminary, and I suddenly realized that I could draw air into my lungs with ease. Due to the profound nature of the spiritual healing, I hadn't even noticed the physical healing. I no longer had to work so hard to catch each breath. I wondered how long the effect would last.

I couldn't wait to go to class two days later to report my good news! I mentioned to my professor, however, that when I drew a breath, it still felt like fire. He offered to pray with me again, but I was hesitant. How could we ask for *more* after God had already done so much?

The professor replied, "Jesus said, 'Whatever you ask for in my name I will do.' He *wants* us to ask." He prayed as he had before, in English and in tongues, and the fire in my lungs immediately went away. To this day it has not returned.

A month later my professor offered to pray with me for some other problems related to my exposure to the toxic mold. As he began to pray over me, asking the Holy Spirit for more grace and more healing, the prayer seemed to intensify. Then something astounding happened. I was thrust backward into the chair by what seemed like a strong wind. I was held there, unable to move or get up, as my professor continued to pray for me. I experienced a tremendous wellspring of grace surging up from within, gushing so fast that I thought I might drown in it.

When the prayer ended I simply said, "I have to go now." A few days later I e-mailed my professor and inquired, "I know that something really big happened. What was that?" He told me about baptism in the Holy Spirit.

All I can say is that since that day, my life has taken a radical turn toward Jesus. I have an intimate and loving relationship with him that I cannot help but share for the sake of the kingdom.

CHAPTER SIX

The Call to Mission

*You shall receive power when the Holy Spirit
has come upon you; and you shall
be my witnesses.*

Acts 1:8

Is God Calling You to Something Today?

—Sharon from Nebraska

When we moved here I longed and prayed for a supportive way to study God's Word intensely, as I had in Michigan. I had two small boys and soon had two more, followed by a cancer diagnosis and another boy! I put my desire for Bible study on the back burner and focused on prayer for restoration of health and for guidance in my vocation as wife and mother to five active sons.

God did not forget my prayer and desire to study his Word. Many years later a woman called me out of the blue. She had just moved to Omaha from Michigan, where she had led a Bible study class. She asked if I was interested in meeting to pray for a class to start in our city. The Holy Spirit sparked joy in my heart, and I leapt at the opportunity to pray with her.

We faithfully met and prayed weekly. God sent two more committed women, so we doubled, and then we quickly doubled again. The time was ripe for us to start a class in our area.

After much prayer and preparation, all was in place. Four women were discerned for leadership positions, and they received further training. I was to be the assistant to the teaching director. We were particularly excited about our teaching director, who had a deep knowledge of Scripture and a heart for prayer.

Training of our local leadership team was to begin in two days, and a regional class director traveled through a blizzard to be with us and bolster us with encouragement and prayer. As our team sat with her around the lunch table, our teaching director announced that she had something to share. We all waited with great anticipation for her wise words.

She told us that she was stepping down. She felt that God was calling her out of the position. The table fell silent. Yet an incredible peace washed over me that was hard to explain. Even with the training sessions only two days away, I felt great peace.

The shocked team went home to pray, agreeing that we would meet later that evening for group prayer. On my way home I turned on the car radio. Catholic radio was on, and Sister Ann Shields, a woman I had known from our days in Michigan, was in the middle of her daily program. It was the feast day of Saint Elizabeth Ann Seton.

Sister Ann read about the miracle of feeding the five thousand. Then she said, "Is God calling you to something today? Is the Holy Spirit prompting you right now to step out in some way? Do you think that God doesn't do this today? *He still does,* and he might be asking you to do something right now. And maybe you don't feel qualified, but when you step out in faith and obedience, *he* will equip you."

I had to pull my car over to the side of the road because I started weeping. It felt as though the Holy Spirit was right in the passenger seat and speaking directly to me. The times are few and far between when I have felt his presence so strongly.

I knew without a doubt that the Lord was calling me to step out in faith and take on the role of the teaching director. He was telling me that he would equip me. Instead of fear I felt peace. I had many reasons why a busy mother of five active boys could not do this, yet I *knew* with certainty that I was to listen to him and act in obedience. There were many hungry women and children already signed up to study his Word. Would he not be our abundant provision?

Since that time God has blessed greatly our young class. In our first six months we have had a hundred women and thirty children coming weekly to study his Word. He has stretched me in a new way that is exciting, though painful at times, as I juggle to do all my tasks well and for the glory of his majestic name.

I had the opportunity to teach this year about the miracle of the feeding of the five thousand as found in Luke 9. God is a God of abundance. He himself is the Bread of Life who came down from heaven. As we listen to him and act obediently, he is well pleased. The Holy Spirit is alive and well in our city and in the hearts of all believers.

I Heard "the Call"

—Tom from Florida

It was early in 1974 when "the thought" seemed to take root. I dismissed it as fantasy. "Me, a preacher of the Word of God? I'm a layman, married with a young family."

It had taken several years to gain a bit of security and benefits in my management position with the company. Besides, I was not even a good conversationalist, let alone a teacher. Indeed, I was an introvert, and one-on-one conversation was a challenge for me. And yet "the thought" persisted, accompanied by a deep desire. I knew that the Word of God had changed my life, and I wanted to share that truth with others.

In time my wife and I discussed the idea, and strangely enough Pam's reaction was, "Yes, this could be from God." Over a period of three months it seemed that the Holy Spirit continued to confirm this word in various ways.

In the midst of this struggle, it occurred to me that if ever I was going to be able to teach the Word, it would require something beyond me. I began to pray and fast and ask the Lord to grant me a gift of teaching.

A few days later Pam and I were invited to a little Christian concert presented by a new group of young people. As they closed the concert, they invited all present to remain there in silence. I sensed the Holy Spirit overshadowing me once again. From within I heard the words, "Tom, you have it!"

At that moment I knew that God had given me the gift of teaching. I knew that I couldn't do it yet, but if I would be faithful to study and then to exercise the gift, God would cause it to grow and would use it for his glory. There was no doubt in my mind about that.

In the early summer it came to light that my company would be leaving the Jacksonville market. I would be transferred, and life could go on as usual. But I knew in my heart that this was decision time. Was God saying, "Tom, leave all that seems to give you and your family financial security"?

That day I had a random encounter that confirmed God's call to me. Leaving work, I steered my car down the spiraling ramp of the multilevel downtown parking garage. As I stopped before the ticket taker's booth, he looked me in the eye and for no apparent reason asked, "Are you a preacher?"

The words rattled me; I knew God was speaking!

The next day I gave my company notice. I had heard "the call," and life would never be the same.

Aren't You Religious?

—*Myra from Michigan*

I was attending a Bible study, and as we studied the Book of Acts, I was very challenged by Paul. During one talk the speaker urged us to pray for more of the Holy Spirit and for his infilling on a daily basis. The next morning I did just that.

Later in the day I attended a parent involvement day at my son's school. During the last class there was only one other parent and myself, and she approached me. "Hi," she said. "Aren't you religious? I heard that from someone."

I told her that God was important in my life and asked her why she wanted to know. She then poured out her life to me, including all of the pain she was going through. I invited her to study the Bible with some women in the neighborhood.

This woman recommitted her life to Christ. She now attends our church, and her daughter attends our youth group and also brings her friends.

I don't think anyone had ever asked me to talk about spiritual things with them. This woman has also taught me things that I needed to learn. I know that the Spirit will bring people to us and give us opportunities to be Christlike.

Renewal Ministries: Lithuania and Beyond
—*Peter Herbeck*

The remaining stories in this book come from some of our experiences with Renewal Ministries, the Catholic mission organization in which we serve. First let me tell you about the miraculous beginnings of this ministry.

In the early nineties Debbie and I had three young children. We felt we were nearing the end of our days of full-time ministry with high-school-age youth, but we weren't sure what was next. I had a strong desire to continue in some type of full-time evangelistic work, but I wasn't sure I could earn enough money to support our family. We placed our concerns and questions before the Lord, looking for some direction from him.

During that season of discernment, Ralph Martin, a friend and mentor, called to ask if I wanted to attend part of a conference with him. He wanted to hear one particular speaker, a prominent pastor who led a large megachurch near Atlanta. I quickly agreed to go.

We attended the morning session, which ended with some general announcements. Since we weren't staying for any more of the conference, we weren't paying too much attention to what was said. The last announcement caught our attention, however: "The team of pastors and prophets on the stage believe the Lord wants us to pray with two men who are here. Those two men are right over there."

The speaker pointed in our direction. I thought he was looking at someone behind us. Once it was clear he was talking to Ralph and me, we agreed to come up for prayer. He excused the rest of the crowd for lunch, and we made our way to the stage.

Members of the prayer team began by praying for Ralph. I was surprised that their simple prophetic words so clearly identified what God was doing in Ralph's life. They said things about him that they could not have known without the help of the Lord.

They then turned to me and began to speak in a similar fashion. Some of their words penetrated my heart like lasers. They seemed to know, in significant detail, exactly what I was going through. They identified with amazing precision my struggles, the specific questions I was asking the Lord and even details about my personal failings and my fears regarding the Lord's will in my life.

Near the end of our prayer, three different people said the Lord was about to open a new set of doors for me. They identified the transition I was in. They then said the Lord was going to open doors to nations around the world and that Ralph and I were a small part of a much larger move of the Holy Spirit in mission in our time. Finally, they said not to try to make it all happen, but wait on the Lord and go through the doors he would open.

Ralph and I left knowing that the Lord wanted our

attention. We decided to take one morning a week to fast and pray, simply to place ourselves before the Lord to listen and to test the words we'd been given. We met weekly for prayer with Sister Ann Shields, one of our longtime friends. Each time we'd discuss what we felt the Lord was saying. For weeks it was nothing more than a sense of encouragement to keep praying.

Finally, after a month or so, Sister Ann mentioned at the end of our prayer that she felt the Lord was telling us to go to Lithuania and Ukraine to do evangelistic work. That caught us by surprise. None of us knew anyone in either place, so we decided simply to continue meeting for prayer and to test what we felt the Lord was saying to us.

Within a month we received a phone call from a bishop in Lithuania. He had just been appointed bishop of the diocese of Kaunas, after his release from seven years in Soviet concentration camps following the Communist collapse in 1989. On his return to Lithuania he immediately had begun to mobilize his priests and religious for the reevangelization of the country. He had obtained our names through a set of relational connections, and he wanted us to help him with that work.

One year later we found ourselves in Lithuania with a team of thirty-five people from throughout the United States and Canada, ranging in age from eighteen to eighty-three. We helped organize three different Catholic rallies in three different dioceses in

Lithuania. As a result of the rallies, over five thousand people filled out information cards expressing their desire to return to the church or to enter for the first time. From that day on we've continued to support the fruitful evangelistic work of our brothers and sisters in Lithuania.

Lithuania was the first door that opened in 1992. Since that time we've worked in an ongoing way with Catholic bishops, priests and lay leaders in twenty-seven different countries around the world, and the doors just keep opening.

I am deeply grateful for the faith of those leaders at the conference we attended. Their ministry to us helped guide the hand of the Lord in our lives.

Encouragement in Hungary

In the mid-1990s I helped lead an evangelistic mission team to Hungary, which included a daylong evangelistic rally in a sports arena in the city of Pecs. Our team arrived by bus the night before the rally. The road to the hotel took us right past the sports arena where our rally was to be held. One of our team members suggested we stop there for a few moments to pray for the rally.

The front door of the arena was open, so we all went in. There were about six members of the local set-up crew working on the stage. We went to the back of the arena floor, where Father Michael Scanlan led us in intercessory prayer. As we prayed we almost immediately sensed the presence and power of the Holy Spirit. One of our team members felt the Lord was saying we would be confronting dark powers at the rally the next day and that the Lord was going to set people free from various kinds of bondages.

As we were praying, one of the members of the set-up team slowly made his way back to us. He told us he had been involved in the occult and spiritualism for more than twenty-five years. He asked for prayer to be freed from the terrible spiritual bondage and oppression he experienced as a result of this involvement. A team member prayed with him, and the man experienced the power of the Lord lifting the oppression.

That simple encounter set the tone for what we were to experience the next day at the rally. It turned out to be one of the most dynamic we've ever done. Two simple things happened to me that I won't forget.

Halfway through the day a crew from the local television network showed up. Just a few years earlier the Communist government had been running this network. The anchor of the crew asked me to do an on-camera interview. Two of his questions were, why were there so many people at the rally, and why did they all seem so joyful? I shared with him a few things from the talks, and then I commented about the fact that joy comes from encountering Jesus Christ in the power of the Holy Spirit.

At the end of the interview, the anchor said he wanted that kind of joy in his life. He was not a believer and had never been baptized. He shared a number of problems he was having in his family that were heavy burdens for him. He asked me if I would pray with him. I laid my hand on his shoulder and simply asked him to invite the Lord to come. As I prayed the Lord touched him, and tears began to flow down his cheeks.

At that point one of our team members came and told me I was needed back on stage for the next session. I grabbed my interpreter, and we hurried toward the stage. As we made our way through the crowd, a young priest who knew my interpreter stopped her. I stood there somewhat impatiently as they spoke to each other in Hungarian.

As I was looking at the priest, I sensed the Holy Spirit telling me that the new mission he was considering for his life was from the Lord. When my interpreter communicated this to the priest, his face lit up. He had come to the rally with one question on his heart. He felt led to get involved in full-time work with youth, but he wasn't sure if it was the Lord calling and if the timing was right for him. Earlier in the day, while I was giving my talk, he had placed his question before the Lord. Then he had said, "If this new ministry is from you, please have Peter come and tell me."

I was stunned. I had never met this priest before. The Lord worked in this simple way to lead him into an important ministry in the church. He left that day filled with encouragement and confidence in God's call on his life as a priest.

A Bishop From Sudan

One morning a few years ago, I was sitting at my desk going through my mail when I came across a letter from Bishop Macram Gassis of Sudan. It was a heartfelt appeal for money to help free girls and boys, many of them Catholic, who had been taken as slaves by Muslim military leaders who had ransacked their villages. The letter moved me to tears. I wrote out a check and sent it in immediately.

For weeks I couldn't get the bishop and the young people out of my mind. Around that time one of our mission leaders at Renewal Ministries called me to say he felt the Lord was calling us to go to Sudan. I told him of my experience and suggested we continue to pray and wait to see what doors the Lord would open for us.

A month later I was leading a mission team in Kenya. We were staying at a retreat center run by religious sisters. One morning, halfway through our stay, I went to the cafeteria for breakfast. I noticed a bishop and a group of priests sitting together at a table at the other end of the room. After my meal I walked by them to offer a greeting.

For some reason the bishop looked familiar to me. I reached out to shake his hand, and he introduced himself as Bishop Gassis from Sudan. He was the bishop who had sent the appeal letter. I told him about the effect his letter had upon me and of our desire to help his cause and to send mission teams to Sudan if possible. He invited me to join him later that day in his office. He allowed our team to tape a television interview with him, which we later broadcast on Renewal Ministries' weekly television program, *The Choices We Face*.

Months later I was feeling that the Lord had more for us to do in Sudan. Two of our team members, Lloyd and Nancy, were on their way to a short-term mission in Uganda. I asked them to inquire whether our friends in Uganda had any contacts in Sudan.

In Uganda Lloyd and Nancy stayed at the Emmaus Center, a wonderful center of evangelistic training and leadership formation. There our friend Joseph told Lloyd that a key leader in Sudan, Bishop Paride Taban, was a friend and occasional visitor to the Emmaus Center. The bishop lived in the hills with his people, who were forced to live like nomads because of the attacks and bombings orchestrated by the Sudanese government. Unfortunately, Joseph had no way of contacting the bishop or of knowing when he was coming to the Emmaus Center again.

About an hour after their conversation, Joseph came rushing into Lloyd's room. "You'll never guess who's here," he said. "Bishop Taban just drove into the compound and will be spending the night. He wants to meet you."

Lloyd and Nancy spent the next few hours talking and praying with Bishop Taban. He invited them to come to Sudan and to help him direct retreats, provide leadership training and assist him in his work of restoration and healing of his people. Lloyd and Nancy now have led numerous missions into Sudan on behalf of Renewal Ministries, and they continue to work closely with Bishop Taban.

A Team to Kazakhstan

Over the past ten years Renewal Ministries has helped lead a large annual Catholic evangelistic rally in Presov, Slovakia. Each year six thousand or so people of all ages cram their way into an old sports hall for a day of worship, preaching, prayer ministry and much celebration. Each year the rally is a dynamic experience of the presence and power of the Holy Spirit.

The primary organizer of the event is Sister Helena. She has lived a heroic life as a nun, including very effective leadership in the underground church during Communist rule. She has played a key role in mobilizing one of the most effective cross-generational Catholic evangelistic efforts I've ever seen. She's a leader; in fact, she has a way about her that makes it difficult to say no to her.

One year, after finishing the annual rally, Sister Helena and I were traveling together to the airport for my departure flight to the United States. On the way we spoke about all the wonderful things that had happened at the rally. She thanked me profusely but then went on to say to me, "Before you leave I'd like to tell you about ten other things we'd like you to help us with over the next few years."

One of the things she mentioned was helping sisters of her order in Kazakhstan with their evangelistic efforts. She said that young Muslims would often ask the sisters questions about Jesus. The sisters felt ill-equipped to respond to the growing opportunity on their own and were asking for help.

Sister Helena told me that Kazakhstan, a mission territory for the Catholic church, was about to get its first diocese. The first Catholic bishop in the history of the country had just been sent to establish the diocese in Karaganda. Sister Helena thought this was a perfect opportunity for Renewal Ministries to serve the church in the former Soviet Union. I told her I would pray about it and get back to her.

On the plane ride home, I prayed over the list of requests Sister Helena had given me. The Kazakhstan opportunity began to take hold of my heart. I sensed the Lord giving me the nod to pursue it. I considered who from our team would be best to send to Kazakhstan. Dr. Peter Williamson, a good friend, Scripture scholar and longtime lay leader in evangelism, came to mind.

On my return home I called Peter. We exchanged greetings, and I began to tell him I had something for him to consider. He interrupted me and said that first he had something exciting to tell me.

Peter had returned a day or two earlier from Rome, where he was completing his doctoral work in Scripture. On his last day there a priest friend introduced him to a young priest from Kazakhstan. This young priest was going back to Kazakhstan to become rector of the first Catholic seminary in the history of the country. He and the new bishop—the one Sister Helena had told me about—were going to leave the next day for Kazakhstan to get things started.

Peter said they spoke for some time, and after Peter shared a bit about our work, the priest pleaded with him to consider bringing a Renewal Ministries team to Kazakhstan. Peter thought we should send a team to Kazakhstan as soon as possible.

I told Peter, "You're never going to believe this. I'm calling to invite you to go to Kazakhstan!"

He said, "You're kidding me, aren't you?"

I said, "No, it's true." I told him all about my conversation with Sister Helena.

Less than a year later Peter was in Kazakhstan helping lead a retreat for more than twenty missionary priests from throughout the country, who were meeting their new bishop for the first time. Since then Peter and others from Renewal Ministries have played a key role in helping develop a growing work of Catholic evangelization in that country.

A Nursing Home in Turkey

Nancy from Texas

On a recent mission trip to Turkey, some nuns who run a nursing home asked us to come and pray for them and the residents. We didn't know how our charismatic style of prayer would be received.

After Mass the priest asked if any of the residents or staff wanted prayer. Those who wanted prayer were to stay in the pews, while the others were free to leave. Most stayed, even though it was lunchtime. The team began to move among the residents and pray with them.

One of our team members felt led by the Holy Spirit to go up to the third floor of the home. As she began to minister, she discovered that the residents on that floor only spoke French. She has a master's degree in French and had lived in France for a year. The Holy Spirit had drawn the only one of us who spoke French there to minister. God handles every detail!

The Holy Spirit led me to a nun from Nigeria who spoke excellent English. As I led her in a prayer, she renounced witchcraft and involvement with the witch doctors to whom her parents had taken her when she was small. She then forgave those who had abused her as a child.

When the conversation led to the gifts of the Holy Spirit, she said that she wanted to speak in tongues. I could see the faith and expectation in her eyes.

After a bit of explanation and prayer, she burst out in a beautiful prayer language. The joy of the Holy Spirit and the gifts seemed to bubble out of her.

After the team was finished praying for everyone in the chapel, we walked through the multistoried building and prayed for those who weren't ambulatory. The mother superior asked some of us to pray a blessing over the kitchen and for the kitchen staff. There had been an outbreak of stomach problems recently, and they wanted God's help to bring it under control.

As we were walking back, I was talking to the beautiful Irish mother superior. We talked about blocks to receiving all that the Holy Spirit wants for us. She asked, "Would you pray for me right now? I'm hungry for all the gifts." We went to her office, and she cried for joy as the Holy Spirit set her free from years of bondage.

The mother superior told me that she and four other sisters of the convent had risen at midnight for the nine days prior to Pentecost Sunday to pray a novena to the Holy Spirit. On Pentecost they had prayed, "Come, Holy Spirit," and they had received a manifestation of the presence of the Holy Spirit but not the gift of tongues. They had really wanted that gift, and they had continued to meet at midnight and pray, "God, please give us the gift of tongues." After we prayed for deliverance, the mother superior received the gift of tongues. God heard her cry.

God not only cares about the big problems that affect people and nations. He also cares for a small group of faithful nuns, in an obscure nursing home, in a country far from the power centers of this world.

Conclusion:
How to
"Walk in the Spirit"

1. Surrender

* The first step is to surrender one's whole life to
  Jesus. The Bible describes full surrender this
  way: "Repent, and be baptized every one of
  you in the name of Jesus Christ for the forgive-
  ness of your sins; and you shall receive the gift
  of the Holy Spirit" (Acts 2:38).

* Repentance here means "conversion." In the
  words of Pope John Paul II, conversion is "a
  complete and sincere adherence to Christ and
  his Gospel through faith.... From the outset,
  conversion is expressed in faith which is total
  and radical.... Conversion means accepting,
  by a personal decision, the saving sovereignty
  of Christ and becoming his disciple."[1]

✶ A key aspect of repentance is making a break with serious sin and the habit patterns of sin in one's life. Going to confession is an essential and practical way to express repentance and to avail oneself of the saving power of Christ.

2. Welcome the Spirit

✶ The Bible instructs us to "earnestly desire the spiritual gifts" (1 Corinthians 14:1). To desire the gifts means to ask for them and to trust that the Lord, who is good, will give them. Jesus himself said, "If you then, who are evil, know how to give good gifts to your children, how much more will the heavenly Father give the Holy Spirit to those who ask him!" (Luke 11:13).

✶ It is important not to ask only once but to express our genuine hunger for the Spirit by means of a daily prayer of petition. Cry out to the Holy Spirit each day! Give the Holy Spirit permission to lead you wherever he desires.

3. Go to the Sources

✶ The daily, prayerful reading of the Bible and frequent reception of the sacraments are essential parts of walking in the Spirit. Each of these is a unique source of the life and power of the Holy Spirit.

* Some parishes offer courses, like the Life in the Spirit Seminar or the Alpha Course, specifically designed to help lead people into a fuller life in the Spirit. Millions have experienced life-changing results from these courses.

* There are many helpful books, tapes, CDs and DVDs available at local Catholic bookstores or from ministries such as Renewal Ministries (www. renewalministries.net), ChristLife (www. christlife.org) and Chariscenter (www.nsc-charis center.org).

4. Fellowship

* One of the most important ways to grow in the life of the Holy Spirit is to share that life with others. One of the authenticating signs of the Holy Spirit's presence is a growing desire to live in communion with other disciples whose hearts are set on following Jesus. That communion is most fully present in the Catholic church, founded by Christ and uniquely equipped through its life, teaching and sacraments to produce a mature life in the Spirit.

* Growth in the Spirit happens best in an environment of lively faith, where everyone welcomes the full working of the Holy Spirit.

5. Obey the Holy Spirit

* If we want to learn to "walk in the Spirit," then
  we must be willing to obey the Spirit's promptings. The Bible tells us, "Do not quench the Spirit,
  do not despise prophesying, but test everything;
  hold fast what is good" (1 Thessalonians
  5:19–21).

* Once we know it's the Spirit who is speaking
  to us, we need to obey his promptings.
  Through prompt obedience to the Spirit we
  learn to hear his voice with increasing clarity
  and depth.

6. Be Missionary

* Pope John Paul II reminded all the baptized:
  "The Church always remains…'in a state of
  mission (*in statu missionis*).' The missionary
  character belongs to her very essence…
  because the Holy Spirit has made her missionary from her origin." Quoting from *Ad Gentes
  Divinitus*, the Decree on the Church's Missionary
  Activity, John Paul continued: [The Spirit]
  comes to instill "into the hearts of the faithful
  the same mission spirit which impelled Christ
  himself."[2]

* The Holy Spirit comes as one who is sent. He
  is the primary agent of the church's evangelistic mission. The Spirit allows the kingdom of
  God to spread throughout the world one heart

at a time. The church exists for this purpose: to cooperate with the Holy Spirit's work to "make disciples of all nations" (Matthew 28:19). To "walk in the Spirit" means to make the Holy Spirit's missionary priorities our own. Ask the Holy Spirit to give you his passion for the salvation of souls. Your heart will soon beat in fuller harmony with the heart of Jesus in the Holy Spirit.

Prayer to the Holy Spirit

Come, Holy Spirit,
  fill the hearts of your faithful
  and enkindle in us the fire of your love.
Send forth your Spirit
  and we shall be created.
And you shall renew the face of the earth.

Let us pray:
O God, who by the light of the Holy Spirit
  did instruct the hearts of your faithful,
  grant that by the same Holy Spirit
  we may be truly wise and ever rejoice in his
  consolation.
Through Christ our Lord. Amen.

Notes

Foreword

1. See, for example, Pope John Paul II's homily at the Solemn Opening of the Second Year of Preparation for the Jubilee, November 30, 1997, no. 3, at www.vatican.va.

2. Pope John Paul II, Speech for the World Congress of Ecclesial Movements and New Communities, nn. 3, 4, 5, in "This is the day the Lord has made! Holy Father holds historic meeting with ecclesial movements and new communities," *L'Osservatore Romano*, English Language Edition, June 3, 1998, pp. 1–2.

Introduction

1. Kilian McDonnell, *The Other Hand of God: The Holy Spirit as the Universal Touch and Goal* (Collegeville, Minn.: Liturgical, 2003), p. 162.

2. McDonnell, p. 165.

Conclusion: How to "Walk in the Spirit"

1. Pope John Paul II, *Redemptoris Missio*, On the Permanent Validity of the Church's Missionary Mandate, December 7, 1990, n. 46, www. vatican.va.

2. Pope John Paul II, *The Spirit, Giver of Life and Love: A Catechesis on the Creed* (Boston: Pauline, 1996), pp. 95, 98, 99.